Practical Applications for Criminal Justice Statistics

Criminal Justice titles available from Butterworth-Heinemann

AFRICAN AMERICAN PERSPECTIVES ON CRIME CAUSA-
TION, CRIMINAL JUSTICE ADMINISTRATION, AND CRIME
PREVENTION
Anne T. Sulton, 0-7506-9813-6

THE ART OF INVESTIGATIVE INTERVIEWING
Charles L. Yeschke, 0-7506-9808-X

COMPARATIVE AND INTERNATIONAL CRIMINAL JUSTICE
SYSTEMS
Obi N. I. Ebbe, 0-7506-9688-5

CONTEMPORARY CRIMINAL LAW
David T. Skelton, 0-7506-9811-X

CONTEMPORARY POLICING: PERSONNEL, ISSUES, AND
TRENDS
M.L. Dantzker, 0-7506-9736-9

CRIMINAL INVESTIGATION: LAW AND PRACTICE
Michael F. Brown, 0-7506-9665-6

CRIMINAL JUSTICE: AN INTRODUCTION
Philip P. Purpura, 0-7506-9630-3

CRIMINAL JUSTICE STATISTICS
Lurigio, Dantzker, Seng, Sinacore, 0-7506-9672-9

THE JUVENILE JUSTICE SYSTEM: LAW AND PROCESS
Mary Clement, 0-7506-9810-1

LAW ENFORCEMENT: AN INTRODUCTION
William Doerner, 0-7506-9812-8

PRACTICAL APPLICATIONS FOR CRIMINAL JUSTICE
STATISTICS
Dantzker, Lurigio, Seng, Sinacore, 0-7506-9830-6

Practical Applications for Criminal Justice Statistics

Edited by:

M. L. Dantzker
Georgia Southern University

Arthur J. Lurigio
Loyola University, Chicago

Magnus J. Seng
Loyola University, Chicago

James M. Sinacore
University of Illinois, Chicago

Butterworth-Heinemann

Boston • Oxford • Johannesburg • Melbourne • New Delhi • Singapore

Library of Congress Cataloging-in-Publication Data
M. L. Dantzker . . . [et al.].
    p.   cm.
    Includes bibliographical references and index.
    ISBN 0-7506-9830-6 (pbk. : alk. paper)
    1. Criminal justice, Administration of—Research.   2. Criminal
justice, Administration of—Statistical methods.   I. Dantzker, Mark L.,
1958–   .
HV7419.5.P73   1997
364'.07'27—dc21   97-9588
                                              CIP

British Library Cataloguing-in-Publication Data
A catalogue record for this book is available from the British Library.

The publisher offers special discounts on bulk orders of this book.
For information, please contact:
Manager of Special Sales
Butterworth–Heinemann
225 Wildwood Avenue
Woburn, MA 01801–2041
Tel: 617-928-2500
Fax: 617-928-2620

For information on all Focal Press publications available, contact our World Wide
Web home page at: http://www.bh.com

10 9 8 7 6 5 4 3 2 1

Printed in the United States of America

Table of Contents

Dedication and Acknowledgments

This text is dedicated to all those individuals who have provided each of us with guidance, support, and love, both in the past and present. Without those individuals, we would not have been able to persevere and succeed. We are eternally grateful to our parents, spouses, and other loved ones too numerous to mention. We would also like to thank those who helped us achieve the final production of this work: Laurel DeWolf, Acquisitions Editor; Stephanie Aronson, Assistant Editor; Maura Kelly, Production Editor; and, of course, all the contributing authors.

Introduction

For many years, university and college teachers have conducted research in their areas of interest and expertise. In addition to gathering further knowledge of the research area, one of their major objectives is to write and publish the results of such research, often in recognized scholarly journals. This exercise not only broadens the researcher's knowledge, but enlightens anyone who may read the published results. Unfortunately, criminal justice students, particularly undergraduates, are seldom readers of such publications unless they need to write a "research" paper or "literature review," or have courses in which issues texts or "readers" are required. Still, even when students are required to read these works, whether or not they actually understand the statistical component of such works is questionable. Therefore, in an effort to improve students' understanding of statistics and how they are used in research, we offer this text, *Practical Applications for Criminal Justice Statistics*, which is composed of ten examples of research conducted by criminal justice academics and practitioners depicting a wide range of statistical techniques used for studying various issues and problems in the criminal justice system.

Textbooks are regularly written that provide students with the theoretical or "how to" approaches on a given subject, such as criminology or statistics. However, due to the applied, social science nature of criminal justice, straight theory or "how to" books are often remiss in providing students with a "realistic" or "practical" outlook. In our textbook, *Criminal Justice Statistics: A Practical Approach*, we pulled theory and "how to" together in a realistic and practical manner that allows students to see the application and importance of statistics in the field of criminal justice. Yet we were not able to fully address statistical usage. In particular, we believe that students should not only see the practical application of statistics but also the scholarly and academic use of statistics, such as in research conducted by criminal justice academicians. *Practical Applications for Criminal Justice Statistics* attempts to remedy that problem.

The articles presented discuss a variety of issues or problems related to criminal justice. They were chosen from a broad field of both previously and never before published research. With the exception of the opening chapter, "The History of Criminal Justice Statistics: A Cautionary Tale," the remaining chapters emphasize a particular statistical technique and its use to study the given issue or problem. In addition, a preface at the beginning of each chapter provides a brief explanation as to why the particular technique was used to study the issue identified. Overall, we believe that *Practical Applications for Criminal Justice Statistics* is not only an excellent companion to our text *Criminal Justice Statistics: A Practical Approach*, but could also be used as a reader for research and special topic courses. We trust you'll agree.

M. L. Dantzker
Arthur J. Lurigio
Magnus J. Seng
James M. Sinacore

The History of Criminal Justice Statistics: A Cautionary Tale

Patricia Loveless

> *Governments are very keen on amassing statistics. They collect, raise them to the nth power, take the cube root and prepare wonderful diagrams. But you must never forget that every one of these figures comes in the first instance from the village watchman, who just puts down what he damn pleases.*
>
> Sir Josiah Stamp (Galvin and Polk 1982, 145)

"Counting," according to Eric Monkkonen, "is the major means of understanding crime and criminal justice in the present . . . we all begin by conceptualization of categories and then ask, 'how many?'" (1980, 53). Today, every facet of the criminal justice system relies on statistics. Police departments allocate officers according to complex statistical models that not only track but also predict the incidence of crime. Corrections officials use complicated statistical models generated by computers to predict prison populations, and governments allocate millions of dollars to build new prisons based on these projections. Politicians' careers rise or fall based on movements in the Uniform Crime Reports. Statistical data has become part of the foundation and fabric of criminal justice in the United States today. Despite this, there are a number of deep-seated and fundamental problems with the collection and analysis of criminal justice data, problems which have existed for hundreds of years and persist to the current time. Therefore, it is extremely helpful for students of Criminal Justice to have some basic knowledge of statistics. Yet, some may ask, Why?

WHY STUDY STATISTICS?

The statistical interpretation of data is a relatively modern phenomenon. The word "statistics" came into usage in the English language only about 250 years ago, and the modern science of social research is scarcely more than a century old. Yet its importance can hardly be overemphasized, for the advent of statistics represented a significant shift in thinking about human behavior. Once such things as plague deaths and crime began to be measured and counted, they became possible to predict and, some believe, even to control. That is the goal of criminal justice statistics today: to aid in predicting and thus preventing and controlling crime.

This book has been created to help reinforce for you what criminal justice statistics are and how they are used with respect to research in criminal justice. Understanding this, however, will not tell you where they came from and why we have them. Therefore, before you read on and see how statistics are applied to research, this chapter sets the foundation for statistical usage by tracing the history of modern statistics to its seventeenth-century English and German roots, discussing the origin of official crime statistics in the United States, describing the problems encountered with official data and efforts to correct these problems, and providing an overview of the current status of crime statistics and statistical research. Monkkonen's concept of "counting" has become fundamental to modern criminal justice administration; this chapter will tell you how this came about. The remaining chapters will show you how particular statistical techniques have been employed in criminal justice research.

EARLY HISTORY OF STATISTICS

"Statistics" comes from the medieval Latin word *statis*, meaning nation or state. Originally, it denoted a comparison, not necessarily numerical, of states and their attributes. For example, Aristotle's *Politeiai*, which was intended as a contribution to his theory of the state, contained descriptions of 158 states, comparing them on such dimensions as history, present character, relations to neighboring states, public administration, justice systems, science and arts, religious life, and manners and customs.

In 1749, the German university professor Gottfried Achenwald translated the Latin word into German as "Statistik," meaning "the political science of individual countries." The English word "statistics" first appeared in W. Hooper's 1770 translation of a German book; it was first used in an English work in 1787, when German statistician E. A. W. Zimmerman published his *Political Survey of Europe* in English. In 1798, the word became firmly established in English through the publication of John Sinclair's *Statistical Account of Scotland* (Cullen 1975). Sinclair was so successful in inserting this new word into the English language that the 1797 edition of the *Encyclopaedia Britannica* included the term statistics, defined as a "word lately introduced to express a view or survey of any kingdom, county, or parish" (Cullen 1975, 10–11).

Seventeenth and Eighteenth Centuries: Two Schools

During the seventeenth and eighteenth centuries, two schools of statistics emerged in Europe, one emphasizing numerical enumeration and the other stressing what we would now call qualitative data. The German school categorized political variables with the goal of improving public administration, while the English school concentrated on what came to be called "political arithmetic," or demographic statistics.

The German school consciously rejected quantification of the variables it examined. Its major architect, Herman Conring

(1606–81), argued that for the state to act rationally, it must have adequate facts upon which to base decisions, and that cross-national comparisons were essential. His approach, illustrated in lectures that he sprinkled with "numerous quotations but no numerical observations," was cultivated by a line of German university professors who were known as the Gottinger School of University Statistics. These men, primarily jurists, collected facts about nations, especially their geography. Information concerning finance, commerce, and population was difficult to obtain at the time, but the German statisticians did not even use the numerical data that was available. Gottfried Achenwald, the person who first translated *statis* into German, is generally considered the father of statistical science, despite the fact that his work was not numerical in nature and had little in common with modern statistics. Ironically, it was this very rejection of quantification that led to the decline of the German school, whose only lasting contribution to the science of statistics was its name.

In England, statistics took a more numerical course. The idea of enumeration had been firmly planted in the English consciousness by William the Conqueror, who conducted an exhaustive economic survey of the country, then did a check survey to determine whether the first enumerators' work was adequate. Quantification of social data began in earnest in 1552, with the passage of the "Bills of Mortality," creating a system of "house watchers" who recorded all deaths. This law arose out of the need for a way to keep track of plague deaths, mobilize the population, and contain the spread of the Black Death. By 1538, parish registers were also keeping records of weddings, christenings, and burials. By 1625, this record-keeping had become institutionalized.

While the German School of statistical science was firmly in the hands of academics, the English School owed its development principally to amateurs. The first book that reports and analyzes data from the Bills of Mortality, *Natural and Political Observations Upon the Bills of Mortality*, was published in 1662 by John Graunt (1620–74), a self-taught London haberdasher with no mathematical background who is considered England's first vital statistician. This landmark work opened up new fields of scientific investigation, shed light on subjects previously unnoticed, and cleared up popular misconceptions. For example, while it was generally believed that London, in 1661, had a population of two million, with women outnumbering men three to one, through both mathematical estimates and surveys, Graunt determined that the actual population was little less than one million and was fairly evenly divided between the sexes.

Graunt observed the regularity of statistical data, although he failed to realize that generalizations from a small number of cases (N) were inaccurate. He was the first to calculate empirical probabilities, and he attempted to enumerate a fundamental probability set, despite problems with incomplete and erroneous data. Graunt frequently collaborated with his friend William Petty (1623–87), a sometime surveyor, professor, and former secretary to Thomas Hobbes.

It was Petty who, around 1672, invented the phrase "political arithmetic," by which the statistical movement in Britain was known until the 1830s. While Graunt concentrated on numbers and calculations, Petty's contribution was as theorist. Like the Germans, Petty believed that the purpose of this new science was to promote sound, well-informed public policy (Porter 1986). He was also one of the first in a long line of social statisticians who viewed themselves primarily as reformers, collecting facts to demonstrate the need for and facilitate reform (Cullen 1975). Petty published a series entitled *Essays in Political Arithmetic* over a seventeen-year period (1783–90), using the Bills of Mortality to examine population growth, commerce, and manufacturing in London and in comparison with Paris and Rome. Focusing on population, he suggested a general register of births, deaths, and marriages to keep track of the number of people who were married; the age structure of the population; the distribution of occupations, religions, and wealth in any geographic area; as well as the number of homes, as an indicator of population density (Cullen 1975).

Another significant figure in English "political arithmetic" of the seventeenth century was Gregory King (1648–1712). In addition to his statistical work, King laid out the streets and squares in the Soho district of London, worked as a map-maker, and, as a specialist in heraldry, was employed at coronations and other ceremonies throughout Europe. King's interest in political arithmetic began with the enactment in 1695 of a tax on marriages, births, and burials, the records of which became the raw material for his work (Barnett 1936). Although King wrote *Natural and Political Observations upon the State and Condition of England* in 1696, it was not published until over a century later, thus somewhat obscuring his place as a founder of statistical science. He does hold the distinction of being one of the first political arithmeticians whose living was earned as a public servant; he served as Secretary first to the Commissioners of Public Accompts (accounts), and then to the Comptrollers of Army Accompts, and later as one of the Commissioners to state King William's debts (Barnett 1936).

By the beginning of the eighteenth century, the notion that social trends such as delinquency could be quantified began to be accepted in Europe, due primarily to two factors: the rise of the insurance industry and the belief by mercantilists that analysis of population growth was essential in determining the power and wealth of a state. In 1728, the age of the deceased was added to information collected under the Bills of Mortality, which led to the creation of "life tables," now known as mortality tables, from which life insurance rates could be determined. Such tables were a direct result of Graunt's early probability work and led to the development of the insurance industry, not only in England, but also in France and Holland. "Life tables" were not without problems, however. Because burials in England were conducted and reported by the Church of England, "dissenters" (those people, including Catholics, Quakers, Methodists, and Baptists, who were not members of the Church and not buried by its clergy) were not counted. As early as 1729, William Maitland estimated that, for this reason, nearly 10 percent of the more than 30,000 burials in London each year did not appear in the Bills of Mortality (Cullen 1975).

The English quantitative approach dominated political arithmetic until the early nineteenth century, but this work bore little resemblance to modern statistics. For the most part, English statisticians were interested in facts, not theory, and they determined probability through raw data and experience, not the gaming table approach taught in modern American universities. While Germans could not resist sniping that "the machinations of these [English] criminal political statisticians in trying to tell everything by figures . . . is despicable and ridiculous beyond words" (Salas and Surette 1984, 459), the English political arithmetician John Arbuthnot (1667–1735) was more concerned with spreading the numerical approach, complaining that nations lacking arithmetic were "altogether barbarous, as some Americans, who can hardly reckon above twenty" (Peters 1987, 80). Quantification was not without reservation, however, as some researchers worried that numerical analysis would deteriorate into useless academic exercises, thereby distracting from the practical significance of their work.

The Nineteenth Century: The Beginnings of Modern Statistics

It was not until the nineteenth century that social scientists began the serious analysis of aggregate social data. It was during this period that the basic methods and theoretical concepts later used by the social sciences were developed. It was also during this time that the English term "political arithmetic" was gradually supplanted by the German word "statistics," which became standard usage during the 1830s and 40s, to designate empirical, usually quantitative, social science.

The dominant figure in statistics during the first half of the nineteenth century was Lambert A. J. (Adolphe) Quetelet (1796–1874), a Belgian mathemetician and astronomer. Founder of the "cartographic" school of criminology, Quetelet was also the first social scientist to derive criminological theory from crime statistics. Using statistical methods to support theoretical concepts, he stressed the need for interpretation, rather than simple descriptive reporting, of empirical data.

A man whose life was one of both accomplishment and tragedy, Quetelet was only seven when his father died. He became a math teacher at seventeen after graduating from the Lycee in his home town of Ghent. At nineteen, he became a professor at the newly created University of Ghent and received its first Doctor of Science degree. In 1823, he went to Paris to study observational astronomy, where he was introduced to mathematical probability theory and became convinced of its universal applicability (Salas and Surette 1984). He assisted the Royal Statistics Commission in preparing the Belgian census of 1826, tutored Prince Albert before his marriage to Queen Victoria, and later was influential in establishing the Royal Statistics Society in England, with Albert as its patron.

Quetelet's early statistical work was based on distinguishing between physical and moral population characteristics, and he published two studies based on this division in 1839. After spending the next ten years studying the application of probability theory to questions of public policy, in 1849 he published *Letters Addressed to H. R. H. the Grand Duke of Saxe Coburg and Gotha on the Theory of Probabilities, as Applied to the Moral and Political Sciences.* This work attempted to make statistics understandable to nonscientists, especially policy-makers who needed to use them to determine whether a country possessed sufficient resources to carry out proposed plans, to know which laws needed reforming, and to address current policy issues with an understanding of their history (Quetelet [1849] 1981).

Topics covered in the "moral statistics" section of this book are familiar to modern social scientists: these include observation; the art versus the science of statistics; combining, checking, and using statistical documents; abuses and research bias; and incompleteness and comparability. Quetelet stressed the need for the theoretical interpretation of empirical data rather than simple descriptive reporting; he derived "laws" directly from facts gathered by himself or other researchers, as part of his work using social data to support political goals and scientific theories.

In 1851, Quetelet organized the first International Statistical Congress, which met two years later. Although a primary concern of the many statistical societies that had been formed during the first half of the nineteenth century had been to produce social data that would buttress statisticians' arguments for social change, this Congress focused on methodological rather than political issues and described ten types of social data that should be collected, including crime statistics.

Shortly after the Congress, at the peak of his professional success, Quetelet's life disintegrated. In 1855 he suffered an attack of apoplexy from which he never recovered, and this was followed by the deaths of his wife and daughter. Although he lived for almost two more decades, he was no longer the driving force in the new statistical science and contented himself with pride over the accomplishments of his son, an astronomer.

Several contemporaries of Quetelet also made significant contributions to the emerging field of statistics. Frederic LePlay (1806–82), who had graduated from a polytechnic school rather than a traditional university and was thus excluded from the mainstream of European academic life, nonetheless developed highly innovative case-study data-collection techniques, using the family as the unit of analysis. LePlay devoted much of his life to the painstaking collection, classification, and analysis of data on over 300 working-class families in every European and several Asian countries. The culmination of this work was the publication of *Les Ouvriers Europeans*, a collection of thirty-six monographs describing with careful and exacting analysis the incomes and expenditures of workers in different countries. One of LePlay's major contributions to the field was confronting the great policy problems of the day and the ideologies being propagated concerning them, earning him the everlasting enmity of Karl Marx.

In 1829, Gerry de Champneuf, who collected and analyzed Parisian judicial statistics, became the first author to incorporate cartography into his presentation of statistical materials. In

England, Charles Booth, who wanted to find out both how many poor people there were and what caused poverty and misery, was the first person in that country to couple statistical research directly with policy. A Liverpool shipowner, he spent his own time and money collecting and analyzing facts about critical problems of the working class and making color maps showing the exact distribution and degrees of poverty in London. For his data, Booth both relied on school inspectors (truant officers) who knew every family in their districts and lived among the poor himself.

"Lies, Damned Lies, and Statistics": Crime Statistics in England

The collection of crime statistics in England began as a result of a political controversy over capital punishment. In 1809, Sir Samuel Romilly, who was campaigning for a reduction in the number of capital offenses, found that information about the number of people committed for trial and their sentences was not available. The Home Office began collecting these statistics the next year; Romilly now had his data and the arguments could begin over their significance (Cullen 1975).

From the beginning, there were serious methodological and technical problems associated with the gathering and analysis of crime statistics. In 1828, both the Select Committee on Criminal Commitments and Convictions, and the Select Committee on the Police of the Metropolis, agreed that most of an apparent increase in crime, based on increased commitments to prison, was really due to changes in the classification of offenses and more effective law enforcement (Cullen 1975).

One major caveat against the use of crime statistics was their lack of reliability, due to the unknown amount of unreported crime, or what Henry Lytton Bulwer first described as the "dark figure of crime." In an 1839 article in the *Journal of the Statistical Society of London* entitled "An Inquiry into the Statistics of Crime in England and Wales," Rawson Rawson, editor of the journal and a leader in the Statistical Society of London, warned that the validity of crime reports depended upon the efficiency of police in detecting and reporting crimes, as well as the willingness of victims to prosecute (Sales and Surette 1984). This led to arguments, first heard in 1840, for victim surveys as a check on the validity of official crime figures.

Another problem was the interpretation of statistical data. From the beginning, English political arithmeticians, as well as statisticians in other countries, viewed their work not as objectively reporting conditions, but rather as promoting particular reforms, such as Romilly's campaign against capital punishment. Thus, only data that would support their arguments was collected, and it was interpreted in light of their particular political persuasions. This led to Benjamin Disraeli's famous remark when he was Prime Minister of England: "There are lies, damned lies, and statistics."

In addition, crime statistics were not uniformly available for analysis until after the First World War. Except for France, which maintained records of police activity as early as the 1820s, and England, where crimes known to the police were recorded beginning in 1857, few countries published crime data, because there was little official effort to compile it in an orderly manner. Countries with federal rather than unitary systems of government, such as the United States, faced particular difficulty in this respect.

The Early-Twentieth Century: Statistics in America

One principal figure in American statistics during the first half of the twentieth century was Walter F. Willcox, a university professor and civil servant who became chief statistician in the Washington Census Office, where he pioneered the use of census data to produce special analytical reports on such topics as racial minorities and divorce. Willcox believed not only that statistics was the only new method of studying social problems developed in modern times, but also that statistics was the only method by which social science could be raised to the level of an actual science.

A prolific writer, Willcox published *Studies in American Demography* (1940), the final work of his long career, when he was over 70; a "Bibliography of the More Important Writing of the Author" fills seven pages of an appendix to this work. *Studies in American Demography*, a collection of essays written for someone who is neither a mathematician or statistician, focused on interpretation not methodology—because he believed that the two were inseparable—and used nothing more mathematically sophisticated than frequencies, percentages, distributions, rates, and ratios (Willcox 1940). Willcox's view that the purpose of statistical data is to facilitate progress by providing precise information in place of unverifiable arguments aligns him with the line of European statisticians who believed that the purpose of demographic information was to inform public policy.

About the time that Willcox retired, a young statistician with a Ph.D. from Yale arrived at the Bureau of the Census to take charge of a new sampling program for the 1940 census. He was W. Edwards Deming, the man who later introduced statistical process control to Japanese industry in the 1950s when American manufacturers, faced with no competition at the time, rejected his techniques as time-consuming and unnecessary. After being "discovered" in the United States through an NBC documentary called "If Japan Can . . . Why Can't We?" (first aired on June 4, 1980), Deming's methods finally gained acceptance in American industry during the 1980s, thus providing evidence for Quetelet's theory about the universality of statistical analysis.

CRIME STATISTICS IN THE UNITED STATES

Three factors have always impeded the collection of reliable police and crime statistics in the United States. First, law enforcement is primarily a local activity; there are literally thousands of police departments, with different enforcement patterns and levels of ability and professionalism, throughout the country. Second, criminal codes vary from state to state, making comparability a major problem. Third, Constitutional prohibitions against federal interference bar the federal government from compelling local governments to report crime data. Thus, there was no major attempt to compile national police or crime statistics until the Federal Bureau of Investigation, with the International Association of Chiefs of Police, established the Uniform Crime Reports (UCR) system in 1929.

In 1931, the National Commission on Law Observance and Enforcement, known as the Wickersham Commission after its chairman, summed up the state of numerical information about crime and police activities in its *Report on Criminal Statistics*:

> The eagerness with which the unsystematic, often inaccurate, and more often incomplete statistics available for this country are taken up by text writers, writers in periodicals, newspaper writers, and public speakers speaks for itself . . . Accurate data are the beginning of wisdom . . . and no such data can be had for the country as a whole, nor have they ever been available hitherto with respect to many of the activities of the Federal Government . . . A proper system of gathering, compiling, and reporting of statistics of crime, of criminals, of criminal justice, and of penal treatment is one of the first steps in the direction of improvement (as cited in Dept. of Justice 1982, 3).

In order to improve this situation, the Wickersham Commission recommended establishing a bureau within the Department of Justice that would have responsibility for compiling and publishing statistics about administration of the federal justice system. The Commission also recommended that states play a greater role in "the collection and transmission of statistics for general national purposes" and that a comprehensive plan be developed for crime and criminal justice statistics at all levels of government (as cited in Dept. of Justice 1982, 3). The Wickersham Commission's recommendations were largely ignored, however, and the UCR remained the only national crime statistics available for the next thirty-seven years.

It came as no surprise, therefore, when the next major investigation into the state of criminal justice in the United States reached the same conclusions as the Wickersham Commission concerning statistical information. In its 1967 report, *The Challenge of Crime in a Free Society*, the President's Commission on Law Enforcement and the Administration of Justice again drew attention to the need for improving national criminal justice data, noting that, "The United States is today, in the era of the high speed computer, trying to keep track of crime and criminals with a system that was less than adequate in the days of the horse and buggy" (Dept. of Justice 1982, 4). The Commission linked information management to crime control and emphasized the need for research and evaluation geared toward correcting problems in the criminal justice system. This time, Congress was listening.

The Omnibus Crime Control and Safe Streets Act of 1968 created the Law Enforcement Assistance Administration (LEAA), authorizing it "to collect, evaluate, publish and disseminate statistics and other information on the condition and progress of law enforcement within and without the United States" (Public Law 90–351, Sec. 515b), (as cited in Dept. of Justice 1982, 4). When LEAA created the National Criminal Justice Information and Statistical Service (NCJISS) in 1970, the nation finally had the "bureau within the Department of Justice with responsibility to compile and publish statistics" recommended by the Wickersham Commission nearly forty years earlier (Dept. of Justice 1982).

NCJISS had a two-pronged mission: to assist states and local communities in developing statistical systems, and also to collect, publish, and disseminate statistical data itself. One of its major accomplishments was the National Crime Survey (NCS), carried out by the Bureau of the Census, which began in 1973. This project, originally recommended in England in 1840, represented the first national attempt to gather data on actual victimization, rather than crimes reported to the police. Designed to complement the UCR, the NCS began with monthly interviews of a representative sample of 5,000 households and 1,500 businesses nationwide, plus supplemental surveys in the nation's thirty largest cities.

CRITICISMS OF CRIME STATISTICS

Despite the efforts of NCJISS, serious problems with statistical data continued to plague both criminal justice practitioners and researchers. In the 1977 article "The Need for Better Data to Support Crime Control Policy," Eleanor Chelimsky of the MITRE corporation (a Federal Contract Research Center), and later of the General Accounting Office, complained that "there does not presently appear to be any simple answer to the basic problem of crime or recidivism measurement accuracy" (1977, 470).

Chelimsky described three problems with the UCR as a foundation for research or policy determination. First, although UCR data are national in scope, readily available, and generated continuously, they are collected and reported on a voluntary basis by thousands of local police departments and are thus highly fallible measures even of reported crime. Second, UCR data reflect only crimes that have been reported to the police and which the police, in turn, have decided to report. Thus, they reflect not only different reporting patterns between neighborhoods and cities, but also the type and quality of local law enforcement; changes in the UCR may reflect shifts in reporting practices or law enforcement professionalization rather than in the amount of crime. Finally, UCR data are incomplete. Not all communities have participated in the UCR throughout its history, and it does not reflect the "dark figure" of unreported crimes. Therefore, according to Chelimsky, "from police and FBI statistics, it is impossible to know whether crime has increased or decreased" (1977, 447).

Chelimsky found just as many problems with victimization surveys such as the NCS, including size of the sample, accuracy of the data, and possible bias, based on the fact that whole neighborhoods in high-crime areas had refused to be interviewed. Concluding that the UCR and victimization surveys both had drawbacks as measures of crime, she proposed a series of changes in the UCR or expansion of the NCS to remedy the situation (Chelimsky 1977).

UCLA historian Eric Monkkonen raised additional concerns in a 1980 article entitled "The Quantitative Historical Study of Crime and Criminal Justice," which outlined three serious problems with criminal justice data from a research perspective. First, all available data were products of some formal action of the criminal justice system and, as such, might be suspect for any number of reasons. Second, although a wide variety of data was available to researchers, it was not available on tape in machine-readable form, making data collection a time-consuming and expensive task. Echoing Chelimsky, Monkkonen's third point was that there was rampant inconsistency, both among the various sources and within a single source, which meant that certain standard data adjustments could not be made and offense rates usually could not be controlled by age or gender.

Obviously, the creation of NCJISS had not solved all of the problems with criminal justice statistics, and the situation remained, as Col. Adolph Jacobsmeyer, Chief of Field Operations of the St. Louis Metropolitan Police Department, had observed in 1968: "When it comes to crime statistics, the pen is still mightier than the sword." By 1979, Congress was ready to apply a common governmental remedy to persistent social problems: bureaucratic reorganization.

Bureau of Justice Statistics: A New Solution

The Bureau of Justice Statistics (BJS) was created by the Justice System Improvement Act of 1979, which passed with broad bipartisan support in both the Senate and House of Representatives. Of its seventeen Congressionally-mandated responsibilities, three were of most importance for completion: (1) collection and analysis of statistical data concerning crime, juvenile delinquency, and the operation of the criminal justice system; (2) recommending national standards for insuring the reliability and validity of crime statistics; and (3) providing technical and financial assistance to state and local governments relating to crime statistics.

The legislation enabling BJS attempted to address several criticisms that had been leveled at NCJISS. Because many critics believed that the statistics function was not sufficiently independent of day-to-day policy decisions at LEAA, Congress chose to make the BJS Director an independent Presidential appointee, one whose political and employment fortunes were not tied to those of the LEAA Director. Responding to charges that NCJISS staff lacked technical expertise, Congress mandated that the BJS Director be a person with experience in statistical programs.

Congress had high expectations for the new Bureau, including improvements in the gathering and analysis of federal, state, and local criminal justice data, better analysis and interpretation of crime indicators, and better information for criminal justice planners. This last expectation developed in response to a third major criticism of NCJISS, that little or nothing was actually being done with the data it collected. In keeping with these expectations, the dominant norm of BJS became expertise; the professional staff members that were hired generally had backgrounds either as statisticians or systems analysts.

In keeping with its mandate to provide better and more useful information about crime, BJS took over the NCS and, in 1983 and 1988, published the *Report to the Nation on Crime and Justice*. This was a glossy, full-color, graphics-laden analysis of the incidence of crime and the functioning of the criminal justice system, both state-by-state and for the nation as a whole, utilizing data from the UCR, NCS, and various other sources, and written in nontechnical language and targeted toward policy makers at the state and national levels. To encourage the accurate collection of data at the state and local levels, BJS provided generous startup and annual funding, with very few strings attached, for states that were willing to create and maintain Statistical Analysis Centers (SACs).

NCJISS and BJS both had a positive impact on the quantity and quality of statistical information available about crime and the administration of justice in the United States. Although the quality of National Crime Survey (NCS) data had been the subject of continuing investigation and review since its inception (Bailar, Herriot, and Passel 1982), most of the questions raised concerned the same issues of validity and reliability that plague any criminal justice research and, indeed, all of social science research. In her monograph *The Influence of Criminal Justice Research*, Joan Petersilia of the RAND Corporation summed up the improvements: "Systematic data are now available on the nation's crime problems and the state of the criminal justice system. . . . Federal interest and support have fostered the growth of criminal justice research as an empirical discipline that has amassed critical databases, developed new methodologies, and used the most advanced and sophisticated analytical techniques" (1987, 96).

CRIMINAL JUSTICE STATISTICS TODAY

Official crime statistics in the United States today are collected by the Federal Bureau of Investigation, based on data voluntarily submitted by police departments across the country. The Uniform Crime Report (UCR) contains data on offenses known as "Index Crimes," which represent an index of serious offenses, including murder, rape, robbery, burglary, auto theft, and other felony theft offenses. Arson was added to the original list during the 1970s, in response to a perceived epidemic of this offense in northeastern "rust-belt" cities. In addition, the FBI collects information on the total number of crimes reported to the police, crime rates per 100,000 population, violent crime, crimes against property, clearance by arrest, and arrest rates—all of which is published in an annual report, *Crime in the United States*.

While underestimating the total amount of crime by some unknown factor (the "dark figure" of unreported crime), the UCR illustrates the movement of crime types and rates over time, charting increases and decreases, and provides an easy way to compare the incidence of crime in different geographic locations. When law enforcement officials, politicians, and the media discuss "the crime rate," they are referring to UCR data.

The second major source of information about crime in the United States today is the National Crime Victimization Survey (NCVS), conducted by BJS. The nation's second-largest ongoing household survey (after the General Social Survey), NCVS obtains data twice a year from a nationally-representative sample of over 49,000 households and comprising about 100,000 persons. From this data, BJS researchers estimate how many rapes, sexual assaults, robberies, assaults, thefts, household burglaries, and motor vehicle thefts were experienced by United States residents over the age of eleven and within respondents' households each year. This data is further broken down to indicate victimization rates for such groups as women, the elderly, members of minority racial groups, and city dwellers.

The major strength of the UCR is that it provides almost universal geographic coverage of the United States, even though it includes only those offenses reported to the police. The NCVS, on the other hand, offers in-depth information and counts crimes that for one reason or another were never reported to authorities, but its coverage is limited to a stratified sample of households. While using a randomly-drawn stratified sample is a very powerful research method that greatly enhances generalizabilty, it, too, has an error rate. Although the numbers of offenses the UCR and NCVS report do not match, their mapping of crime patterns and trends over time has been remarkably consistent. Taken together, the UCR and NCVS provide a picture of crime in the United States that is both broad and deep.

In addition to crime statistics, the FBI collects and reports data on the number of personnel employed in law enforcement agencies. BJS also gathers data on many facets of the criminal justice system, including courts and corrections. Each year, BJS surveys the nation's court systems, requesting information about both civil and criminal cases and their outcomes. The National Prisoner Statistics (NPS) project produces annual and semiannual data on the number of prisoners held in each state, the District of

Columbia, and the federal prison system; BJS conducts a Census of Jails and a Census of State and Federal Prisons at five-year intervals. Since 1983, the National Corrections Reporting Program (NCRP) has collected data on prison admissions and releases, and on parole entries and discharges, in participating jurisdictions, including demographic information, conviction offenses, sentence lengths, credited jail time, and time served.

A great deal of this information, along with data about the administrative functioning of the criminal justice system, reports on specialized populations such as juveniles in custody, and specialized problems such as drug use, are complied into the *Sourcebook on Criminal Justice Statistics*, which has been published annually since 1972. Finally, BJS issues reports on specific criminal justice issues and problems, such as *Drugs, Crime and the Justice System*.

Much of the statistical research on criminal justice issues in the United States today is carried out by individual academic criminologists, criminal justice professors, and professional researchers who work for government agencies or private "think tanks." One major source of funding for this research is the National Institute of Justice (NIJ), a branch of the United States Department of Justice, whose primary function is to sponsor criminal justice research through grants and contracts and publish the results. Each year, NIJ awards thousands of dollars to scholars to pursue research on topics it deems important.

WHY CRIMINAL JUSTICE STATISTICS?

From a social science perspective, research involving criminal justice statistics has three main purposes: knowledge expansion, operations management, and program evaluation. Researchers in academic institutions, private think-tanks, and government agencies such as BJS on the federal level and SACs on the state level, utilize criminal justice statistics to describe the incidence of crime, devise offender and victim profiles, report patterns of official response, and, in general, tell us things not previously known about crime, criminal behavior, and the justice system. While such studies may or may not have any immediate practical use, they follow the tradition of the German and English schools of thought on statistics, that governments need data to make informed decisions, and that raw, unanalyzed data sets are not particularly useful in this regard.

CONCLUSION

Over two short centuries, statistics has evolved from Sinclair's system of counting the natural and human resources of a country to one which provides the tools necessary for "current and future efforts to improve the lot of humankind" (Rossi and Freeman 1985, 399). From the beginning, statistics has been viewed as a tool for both the expansion of knowledge and the betterment of public policy. The effectiveness of criminal justice research is to a large extent dependent upon the accuracy of the data upon which statistical analyses are performed, and although these still present some problems of incompleteness, inconsistency, and bias, both data accuracy and research methodology have improved greatly since the time of John Graunt and the first Bills of Mortality. This has had an undeniably positive effect on criminal justice policy and practice, especially during the latter half of the twentieth century.

In short, statistics have come to play a major role in crime prevention, analysis, and reporting; in evaluating and understanding differing aspects of the Criminal Justice System; and for conducting a broad body of criminal justice research. The remainder of this text primarily demonstrates how statistics are used in the evaluations and analyses of selected criminal justice related issues and topics.

REFERENCES

Bailar, B. A., R. A. Herriot, and J. S. Passel. 1982. The quality of Federal census and survey data. *Review of Public Data Use* 10:230–218.

Barnett, G. E., ed. 1936. *Two tracts by Gregory King*. Baltimore: Johns Hopkins University Press.

Chelimsky, E. 1977. The need for better data to support crime control policy. *Evaluation Quarterly* 1:439–74.

Cullen, M. J. 1975. *The statistical movement in early Victorian Britain: The foundations of empirical social research*. New York: Barnes and Noble.

Deming, W. E. 1986. *Out of the crisis*. Cambridge: Massachusetts Institute of Technology Center for Advanced Engineering Study.

Galvin, J., and K. Polk. 1982. Any truth you want: The use and abuse of crime and criminal justice statistics. *Journal of Research in Crime and Delinquency* 19:135–65.

Monkkonen, E. 1980. The quantitative historical study of crime and criminal justice. In *History and Crime: Implications for Criminal Justice Policy*, eds. J. A. Inciardi and C. E. Faupel, 53–73. Beverly Hills: Sage Publications.

Peters, W. S. 1987. *Counting for something: Statistical principles and personalities*. New York: Springer-Verlag.

Petersilia, J. 1987. *The influence of criminal justice research*. [Santa Monica]: RAND Corporation.

Porter, T. M. 1986. *The rise of statistical thinking 1820–1900*. Princeton: Princeton University Press.

Quetelet, M. A. [1849] 1981. *Letters addressed to H. R. H. the Grand Duke of Saxe Coburg and Gotha on the theory of probabilities, as applied to the moral and political sciences*. Reprint, New York: Arno Press, 1981.

Rossi, P. H., and H. E. Freeman. 1985. *Evaluation: A systematic approach*. 3d ed. Beverly Hills: Sage Publications.

Salas, L., and R. Surette. 1984. The historical roots and development of criminological statistics. *Journal of American Criminal Justice* 12:457–65.

U.S. Department of Justice. Bureau of Justice Statistics. [1982]. *Bureau of Justice statistics five-year program plan: FY 1982–1986*. Washington, D.C.

Willcox, W. F. 1940. *Studies in American demography*. Ithaca: Cornell University Press.

2

Drug Testing in Community Corrections: A Comparative Program Analysis*

Gennaro F. Vito, Stephen T. Holmes,
Thomas J. Keil, and Deborah G. Wilson

PREFACE

We chose to use discriminant function (bar charts) for several reasons. First, our dependent variable, the drug test result, is nominal (Positive/Negative). Second, discriminant function would develop a profile for each type of drug test that is easily interpret-

* This article was previously published in the *Journal of Crime and Justice*, *XV*(1), 1992, pp. 63–89. It appears by permission of Anderson Publishing Co. and the authors. All rights are reserved. No part of this article may be used or reproduced by any means without permission from the publisher (Anderson). This research was partially supported by a grant from the Bureau of Justice Assistance as well as a research completion grant from the University of Louisville under the sponsorship of President Donald C. Swain. The authors express their gratitude to the staff of Louisville-Jefferson County Crime Commission (Kim Allen, Director), the Louisville Branch Office of the Division of Community Services (Kentucky Corrections Cabinet, James Hager, Branch Manager), and Kentucky Substance Abuse Programs, Inc. (Sam Eyle, Executive Director). The opinions expressed in this article are solely those of the authors.

able by persons not familiar with statistical analysis. The "profiles" would tell the probation/parole officer the basic type of client who is most likely to have a problem with a particular drug. Also, the analysis would let the treatment program know the type of client the treatments were more effective (and least effective) with, so they could adjust their offerings accordingly.

ABSTRACT

This article presents comparative results from the first two years of a drug testing program for probationers and parolees in Louisville, Kentucky. Comparisons are made between the research findings from the first and second years of the program and to the results from the drug use forecasting program (DUF). For both years, marijuana (59% and 53% of all tests) and cocaine (36% and 28%) were the drugs typically abused. Clients who completed the Kentucky Substance Abuse Program (KSAP) were less likely to recidivate. Client attributes associated with substance abuse were established through the use of discriminant function analysis.

INTRODUCTION

Drug abuse among clients has become a dominant concern in community corrections. New programs and approaches are needed to address this crucial issue. The generic model presently in place involves: monitoring of the client through drug testing, identification of the nature of the substance abuse problem, and a thorough assessment and referral for treatment. This supervision strategy makes use of the information provided by continued testing and performance in the treatment program, and close collaboration between officers, clients and treatment providers (Weinman, Bowen & Mueller 1990, p. 51). The TASC model (Treatment Alternatives to Street Crime) provides a diversion program and links community corrections and the drug abuse treatment system. Of course, the drug abuse testing and treatment is coerced—it is ordered by the court or the parole board (Leukenfeld 1990, p. 6). This article presents comparative results from the first two years of such a program in Louisville, Kentucky.

DRUG ABUSE AND CRIME

A strong link between substance abuse and criminal behavior has been demonstrated. Offenders with active drug or alcohol abuse problems are likely to continue their criminal behavior. Drug abuse is highly correlated with frequent criminal activity, including violent crime, habitual offending and delinquency (Blumstein et al. 1986; Chaiken & Johnson 1988; Graham 1987; Gropper 1985; Inciardi 1986; Wish & Johnson 1986). In addition, problem drinking offenders are disproportionately involved in violent crime (Collins 1986).

A survey of state prisoners in 1979 revealed that the inmates demonstrated "an excessive pre-prison involvement with alcohol" and that "illegal drug use is about as pervasive among inmates as alcohol" (Bureau of Justice Statistics 1983a, p. 2, 1983b, p. 5). By 1986, this pattern of inmate substance abuse had worsened (Innes 1988). Thirty-five percent of the inmates admitted that they were under the influence of drugs at the time of their offense. Forty-three percent of the inmates stated that they were using illegal drugs on a daily or almost daily basis before their arrest.

There is evidence that offenders in community corrections also have high rates of substance abuse. A national study (Hubbard et al. 1989) reports that over 30% of the clients in residential and outpatient substance abuse treatment were referred by the criminal justice system. In their study of offenders on intensive supervision in California, Petersilia and Turner (1990) reported that 50% of the clients were in need of drug treatment. Few of these offenders received treatment and eventually they committed new drug-related offenses.

Such findings have led to the increased enforcement of drug laws. As more offenders convicted of drug crimes hit the correctional system, community corrections is forced to deal with the overflow. In fact, if offender drug abuse is effectively treated, community corrections can provide an outlet for prison and jail overcrowding (see Robinson & Lurigio 1990).

TREATMENT PROGRAM RESULTS

Treatment for drug abusing offenders can be effective. A research compendium of 41 treatment programs (Hubbard et al. 1990) reported significant decreases in heroin and cocaine use among clients in treatment for at least three months. In their review of the treatment literature, Gendreau and Ross (1987, p. 385) found that "addicts who stay the course of treatment or re-enroll after initial failure can decrease their drug intake and reduce criminal offenses." Research on the Kentucky Substance Abuse Program (Vito 1989a, 1989b) found that parolees who completed the program had substantially lower reincarceration rates during the first and second year of operations (3.6% and 9.7%) than those who did not complete treatment (35.2% and 36.6%).

These findings underscore the need for effective offender treatment. Drug-testing programs must be coupled with treatment, in addition to punitive sanctions.

DRUG-TESTING PROGRAM RESULTS

The majority of drug testing programs cited in the literature are aimed at the pre-trial releasee population. One of the purposes of these programs is to determine the level of substance abuse in the offender population (see Wish & O'Neil 1989). A number of community corrections programs are presently in place but their results have not been published (see Hadlock 1990; Levy & Meyer 1990).

However, Wheeler and Rudolph (1990) provide detailed results of a program that tracked a sample of felony probationers subjected to drug testing (N = 658) in Houston in 1989. This sample was studied for an eleven-month period and failure was defined as a law violation, probation revocation (due to law or technical violation), a pending revocation, absconder status, or unsuccessful termination. The study determined that probationers who failed tended to be younger drug users with higher risk scores and a greater number of prior felony convictions than successful probationers (Wheeler & Rudolph 1990, p. 40). Probationers who failed drug tests were more likely to fail on probation and drug offenders committed a substantially higher percentage of technical violations. Finally, one unexpected finding was that drug offenders who did not participate in a treatment program had a higher rate of success (57%) versus those who did take part in treatment (43%).

These findings do not compare directly with those reported from the first year of the Louisville drug-testing program (Vito, Wilson, & Keil 1990). As a result of a positive test, 356 of the clients tested were referred to the Kentucky Substance Abuse Treatment Program. Twenty-eight percent (101) completed treatment. Of those who completed treatment, only 3% were reincarcerated by the end of the first program year. The reincarceration rates for clients who were referred but did not complete treatment was 17.5%. This rate was twice as high for clients who tested negative (6%). Obviously, the treatment had an impact on recidivism as measured by subsequent incarceration.

PROGRAM DESCRIPTION

Drug testing programs in community corrections can follow a number of different models (see Bocian & Kempske 1990; Hadlock 1990; Nidorf et al. 1990). The Jefferson County Probation and Parole Office of the Division of Probation and Parole (of the Kentucky Corrections Cabinet) has had a drug-testing program for clients since July of 1989. Funding for this program originated from a federal grant provided by the Bureau of Justice Assistance to the Kentucky Justice Cabinet as a part of the statewide drug strategy. The drug-testing program grant was awarded to the Louisville-Jefferson County Crime Commission with matching funds provided by the Jefferson County Government.

Grant oversight and administration was the responsibility of the Louisville-Jefferson County Crime Commission. An oversight advisory board provides general program guidance and review. Program administration and oversight was provided by the Division of Probation and Parole (Kentucky Corrections Cabinet). The daily program operational management was the responsibility of the branch manager of the Jefferson County Probation and Parole Office. A project coordinator maintained the daily and monthly records necessary to coordinate the program and acted to ensure a smooth coordination of all agencies involved.

The purpose of the drug-testing program was to enhance public safety by establishing a system for the identification of controlled substance abuse among probation and parole clients. Additionally, the program sought to establish information on the nature and frequency of substance abuse in this population. If the test was positive, offenders were referred to the Kentucky Substance Abuse Program (KSAP) for entry into the treatment program until all available slots were filled. Offenders were periodically retested. If the initial test was negative, the offender did not receive a treatment referral. Even those offenders who passed the test were candidates for retesting.

The monitoring goal of the program was translated into two objectives: (1) the testing of all clients beginning community supervision to determine the percentage of these clients with a drug abuse problem ("New Cases"), and (2) random testing of clients presently under community supervision ("Old Cases").

METHODS

During the second year of the project, a total of 1556 clients (on probation or parole) were tested. Every client was tested at least once and some were tested a maximum of five times. Where possible, comparisons were made between the research findings from the first and second years of the program and to the results from the drug use forecasting program (DUF)[1].

Both bivariate and multivariate statistics were used to analyze these data. The multivariate analysis used discriminant analysis to construct profiles of different types of substance abusers revealed by the drug testing. As defined by Norusis (1990, p. 78):

> Descriptive statistics and univariate tests of significance provide basic information about the distribution of variables in the groups and help identify some differences among the groups. However, in discriminant analysis and other multivariate statistical procedures, the emphasis is on analyzing the variables together, not one at a time. By considering the variables simultaneously, we are able to incorporate important information about their relationships.

It is similar to multiple regression (see also, Belknap 1987; Vito, Wilson & Keil 1990; Wheeler & Rudolph 1990).[2] Here, we focus upon the research questions addressed during the second program year.

RESEARCH FINDINGS

What Was the Pattern of Abuse Revealed by the Drug Testing?

There was little variation in the incidence of drug abuse during the first and second year of the program. For both years, marijuana (59% and 53% of all tests) and cocaine (36% and 28%) were the drugs typically abused. The rate was slightly lower during the second year but the rate of abuse for narcotics (2% to 8% of all tests) and stimulants (1% to 9%) increased.

Figure 2.1 presents the rate of positive drug tests across all five tests for the first and second years of the program. Although the rate of abuse was lower on the first test during the second year, the percentage of positives were higher than previously on tests four and five.

Overall, the rate of substance abuse on the initial test was lower during the second year of the program. Yet, this rate increased on subsequent tests to either meet or exceed that of the

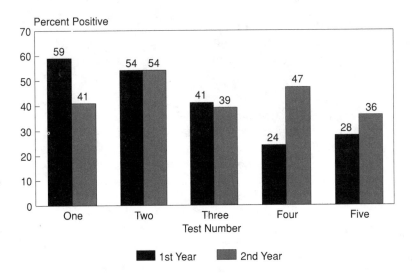

Figure 2.1 Positive Rates on Drug Testing (First versus Second Year).

previous year. For example, the rate of positives on the first test were lower during the second year for marijuana (from 47% down to 30%), cocaine (22% to 15%), and multiple use (more than one drug—17% to 11%). However, Figure 2.2 reveals that the rate of marijuana abuse during the second year met or exceeded that of the first when each test is examined. Figure 2.3 reveals a very similar pattern for cocaine with distinct variation on tests four and five.

What Client Attributes Were Associated with Substance Abuse?

First, we examined the rate of substance abuse on the initial test for the first and second years of the program. Although the rates were lower during the second year, the following patterns were present:

- The positive rate for blacks (71% & 46%) was higher than that of whites (46% & 36%) during both years.[3]

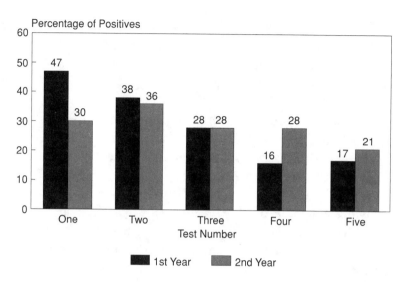

First versus Second Year Results

Figure 2.2 Rates of Marijuana Abuse (All Tests).

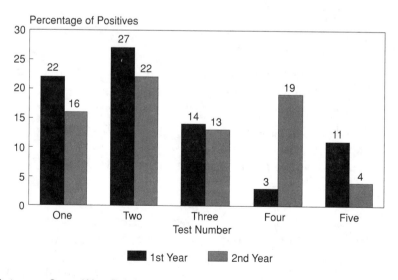

First versus Second Year Results

Figure 2.3 Rates of Cocaine Abuse (All Tests).

- The level of abuse was consistent across gender and age groups and by the type of offense during the second year with no substantial peaks.
- During the second year, shock probationers (57%) had the highest rate of abuse on the initial test.
- For both years, clients with identifiable drug or cross addiction problems had the highest rate of abuse (63% & 47%).
- Clients under maximum supervision had the highest rate during the second year (51%).

A positive outcome on the first drug test during the two years of the program was related to race, type of release (shock probation), clients with an admitted drug problem, and maximum supervision.

The second comparison focused upon the results on the first drug test during the first two years of the program by type of drug. The following patterns were present for *marijuana* abuse:

- Males had higher rates of abuse for both years (48% & 31%) but the difference was somewhat greater in the second year (31% vs. 24%).
- Blacks were more likely to abuse marijuana but the gap narrowed significantly during the second year (58% vs. 36%; 32% vs. 28%).
- For both years, the younger the client, the more likely the abuse of marijuana. The peak age group was 21–29 but this peak was lower during the second year (54% vs. 43%). The rate of abuse was also more evenly distributed across the age groups in year two.
- Shock probationers (36%), rather than probationers (34%, down 14%), had the highest positive test rate for marijuana in the second year.
- Persons who report being cross-addicted (35%), rather than drug addicted (31%), had the highest rate of marijuana abuse in year two.

- Clients on maximum (37%), rather than advanced, supervision had the highest rate of marijuana abuse during the second year.

Males, blacks, persons on shock probation, and persons who were admittedly cross addicted or on maximum supervision were likely to test positive for marijuana.

A second analysis was conducted to outline a cocaine profile. In terms of *cocaine* abuse:

- Females (24% & 17%) and blacks (36% & 25%) had a higher rate of cocaine abuse for the second straight year and by a greater margin (+3% & +20%).
- Unlike the first year, the pattern of cocaine abuse increased with the age of the client (i.e. 40–49: 21%).
- For both years, persons convicted of drug offenses (27% & 18%) had the highest rate of cocaine abuse.
- Shock probationers (29%), rather than probationers (16%), had the highest rate of cocaine abuse in year two.
- Clients with a reported drug problem (30% & 19%) had the highest rate of cocaine abuse in both years of the program.
- In both years, clients under maximum supervision (28% & 20%) had the highest rate of cocaine abuse.

Females, blacks, older clients, shock probationers, those with a confessed drug problem, and clients on maximum supervision were likely to test positive for cocaine. Overall, the drug testing revealed remarkably similar patterns during the first two years.

During the Second Year, Which Variables Predicted Failure on the First Drug Test?

Here, we begin a multivariate analysis (discriminant function analysis) of the factors which predict a positive outcome on the first drug test. In this analysis, it was necessary to subdivide the sample into racial groups for every drug except marijuana. This method was necessary because race was a factor in the outcome on the first test. Although a roughly equal number of blacks (N = 787) and whites (N = 761) were tested, black offenders (58%) were more likely to test positive than whites (42%).

For *whites* the probability of a positive result on the first test was related to the following attributes:

- Drugs, rather than alcohol, were the primary problem identified by the client.
- "Old," rather than "New," Cases.
- Probationers, rather than parolees or misdemeanant probationers.
- The younger the client, the greater the chance of a positive result.
- A fewer number of previous alcohol-related arrests.

In summary, white clients who were positive on the first test had drug problems, were not new to supervision, were probationers, younger on average, and had a low average number of previous alcohol arrests.

For *blacks*, the chance of a positive first test was related to:

- Probationers, rather than parolees or misdemeanant probationers.
- Drugs, rather than alcohol, were the primary problem identified by the client.
- "Old," rather than "New," Cases.

Black clients who failed the first drug test were likely to be probationers, have a drug problem, and already under supervision. Therefore, on the first test, both whites and blacks had three variables in common: probation drug problems, and long-term community supervision.

During the Second Year, Which Variables Predicted Cocaine Abuse on the First Drug Test?

For *whites*, a positive outcome for cocaine on the first test was significantly related to:

- Probationers, rather than parolees.
- Drug abuse, rather than cross addiction, was the primary problem identified by the client.

White cocaine abusers were likely to be probationers with a known drug abuse problem.

For *blacks*, the probability of a positive cocaine first test was related to:

- Drugs, rather than alcohol, were the primary problem identified by the client.
- A drug offense, rather than violent crime, was the present offense.
- "Old," rather than "New," Cases.

Blacks who tested positive for cocaine had an admitted drug problem, had recently committed a drug offense, and were not new to supervision. It appears that there were some significant differences between the racial groups with regard to cocaine abuse but cocaine abuse is linked to a history of drug abuse.

During the Second Year, Which Variables Predicted Multiple Abuse on the First Drug Test?

For *whites*, the probability of multiple drug abuse on the first test increased for:

- Females rather than males.
- The greater the number of prior drug arrests.
- Drug offenders rather than violent or property offenders.

White females, offenders with a higher than average number of drug arrests, and drug offenders were likely to abuse more than one drug.

Black clients were more likely to test positive for more than one drug on the first test when:

- They were probationers, rather than misdemeanant probationers.
- A drug offense, rather than violent crime, was the present offense.

Blacks on probation and those who had committed a drug offense were likely to be multiple abusers of drugs.

During the Second Year, Which Variables Predicted Marijuana Abuse on the First Drug Test?

Here it was not necessary to subdivide the sample by race. The probability of a positive first test for marijuana was related to:

- The younger the client, the greater the chance.
- Probationers, rather than parolees or misdemeanant probationers.
- Drugs, rather than alcohol, was the primary problem identified by the client.
- "Old," rather than "New," Cases.

During the second year of testing, marijuana abusers were likely to be youthful, on probation for some time, and have a known drug abuse history.

How Does the Drug Abuse Pattern Revealed by the Testing Program Compare to That in Other Cities?

This comparison is purely exploratory in nature. Here, the Louisville program rates are compared with proximate cities from the Federal Drug Use Forecasting (DUF) program—Indianapolis, Kansas City, and St. Louis.[4] Figure 2.4 demonstrates that the rate of substance abuse evidenced by the Louisville program was substantially lower than that registered in the other cities under the DUF. However, in Figure 2.5, we see that the rate of marijuana abuse in Louisville was somewhat comparable to that in the DUF cities Yet, the rate of cocaine abuse (Figure 2.6) among

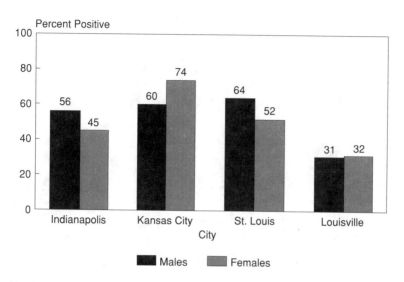

Positive Rates for Any Drug by Sex

Figure 2.4 Rates of Drug Abuse (DUF Cities vs. Louisville).

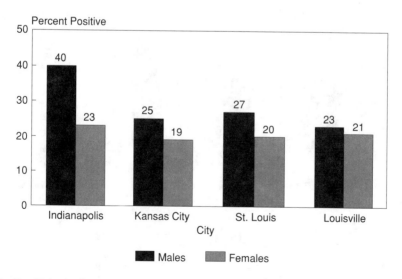

Positive Rates by Sex

Figure 2.5 Rates of Marijuana Abuse (DUF Cities vs. Louisville).

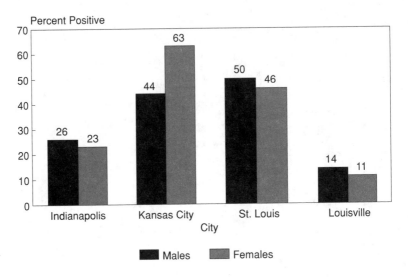

Positive Rates by Sex

Figure 2.6 Rates of Cocaine Abuse (DUF Cities vs. Louisville).

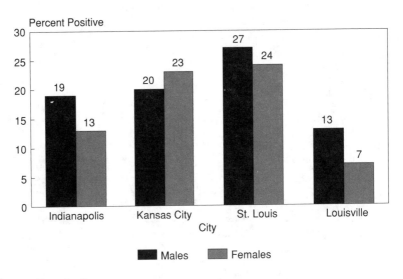

Positive Rates by Sex

Figure 2.7 Rates of Multiple Drug Abuse (DUF Cities vs. Louisville).

the Louisville clients was substantially lower than that in the DUF cities Finally, Figure 2.7 demonstrates that the level of multiple drug abuse was demonstrably lower in Louisville in comparison with the DUF cities.

On the basis of this information, it would appear that the substance abuse problem in Louisville is substantially different than that in other neighboring cities. Overall, the rate of substance abuse in general and for cocaine and multiple abuse in particular, is much lower in the Louisville testing group. Yet, marijuana abuse rates are comparable to the other cities. However, we must emphasize that the DUF program represents both a very different population and method of testing.

What Was the Recidivism (Reincarceration & Revocation) Rate for Offenders Who Tested Positive and Were Referred to Treatment Versus Those Who Were Negative for Drug Abuse?

At this point, we compare the reincarceration rates of the clients tested. The KSAP group is subdivided into two parts: 1) those clients who completed the program ("Graduates") and 2) those who did not complete the program ("Exits"). It must be recalled that KSAP does not control client entry to nor exit from treatment. This decision lies entirely with the probation/parole officer. The officers make the referral to the program and then they determine whether or not the client should remain in treatment. The third group consists of clients who were tested but not referred to KSAP ("Kontrols").

Of course, this comparison is imperfect because it does not include an experimental design with clients assigned at random for both testing and treatment. Therefore, an analysis of the three groups was conducted in order to determine if the three groups were comparable. The results of this analysis are presented in Table 2.1.

In all, there were six statistically significant differences between the three groups. First, it is obvious that the clients referred to KSAP (both Graduates and Exits) were far more likely to have positive results on the first test. This result is not unexpected. After

Table 2-1 Significant Differences Between the Groups Involved in Jefferson County Drug Testing Program.*

Variable	KASP Graduates	Type of Group KASP Exits	Kontrol
Result on 1st Test:			
Positive	116	264	106
	(100.0%)	(97.8%)	(9.1%)
Negative	0	6	1064
	(0.0%)	(2.2%)	(90.9%)
Positive Result on 1st Test for:			
Marijuana	85	113	48
	(73.3%)	(42.8%)	(45.3%)
Cocaine	12	55	19
	(10.3%)	(20.8%)	(17.9%)
Multiple Drugs	101	188	71
	(87.1%)	(71.5%)	(67.0%)
Race:			
White	58	106	597
	(50.0%)	(39.7%)	(51.2%)
Black	58	161	568
	(50.0%)	(60.3%)	(48.8%)
Type of Case:			
"Old" Cases	71	158	463
	(61.7%)	(59.2%)	(39.9%)
"New" Cases	44	109	697
	(38.3%)	(40.8%)	(60.1%)

* In addition to the differences listed here, an examination using Anova and multiple classification analysis determined that 1) the Exit group was younger than Graduates or Kontrols, and 2) Graduates had a higher average number of prior drug arrests.

all, the KSAP referral was reserved for clients who tested positive. Consequently, the KSAP clients (either the Graduates or the Exits) had higher positive rates for marijuana, cocaine, or multiple drugs on the first test.

In terms of race, there was a substantially higher percentage of blacks in the Exit group (60%). Finally, the KSAP groups had a greater proportion of clients who fit the testing guidelines ("Old Cases"). In addition, it was discovered that the Exit group was younger than the other two groups and that Graduates had a higher than average number of prior arrests.

Due to the fact that the three groups were different in nature and construction, a multivariate analysis (discriminant function analysis) was conducted to more accurately compare recidivism rates. The following attributes determined which of the clients returned to prison:

- The greater the number of positive tests for cocaine, the greater the likelihood of reincarceration.
- The greater the number of positive tests for marijuana, the greater the likelihood of reincarceration.
- Parolees, rather than probationers, were more likely to be reincarcerated.
- Exits, rather than Graduates or Kontrols, were more likely to be reincarcerated.

The multivariate results confirmed that the Exit group, despite the differences between the three groups, had the highest rate of recidivism.[5] If clients with a substance abuse problem completed KSAP, they were less likely to be reincarcerated.

Of course, reincarceration was tied to the revocation process. It is possible that the Exit group, after their removal from KSAP, were prime candidates for revocation. Were they returned to prison because they failed in KSAP and demonstrated continual problems with substance abuse?

This question was addressed in another multivariate analysis which addressed the probability of revocation. The discriminant function analysis revealed that:

- The greater the number of positive tests for cocaine, the greater the likelihood of revocation.
- Parolees, rather than probationers, were more likely to be revoked.
- The greater the number of positive tests for marijuana, the greater the likelihood of revocation.

- Clients on intensive, rather than advanced, supervision were more likely to be revoked.

Three of the same variables predicted the probability of reincarceration and revocation. The differences were the factors intensive supervision and completion of KSAP. Clearly, removal from KSAP did not automatically lead to a revocation of the supervision period and a return to prison for that reason. Exits were not more likely to be revoked than either Graduates or Kontrols.

What Factors Were Related to the Completion of the Treatment Program (KSAP)?

This analysis should provide some indication of the type of client most likely to complete the treatment program. The following variables predicted completion of KSAP:

- The lower the number of positive tests for cocaine, the less likely the client was to complete KSAP. In other words, clients who tested positive for cocaine were unlikely to complete the treatment program.
- Parolees, rather than probationers, were more likely to complete KSAP.
- Probationers, rather than misdemeanant probationers, were more likely to complete KSAP.
- Clients under intensive, rather than maximum or advanced, supervision were more likely to complete KSAP.
- The older the client, greater the likelihood of KSAP completion.

Perhaps the most important variable is the first—clients with severe cocaine abuse problems were less likely to complete KSAP. The implication is that treatment of the cocaine client was difficult to accomplish under the KSAP regimen. As a result of this finding, KSAP officials decided to treat cocaine abusers as a separate group, hold meetings more often, and retest them frequently. The results of this specialized treatment will be examined in the third-year program evaluation.

CONCLUSIONS

Some general policy statements can be made on the basis of this research. First, it appears that the Jefferson County Drug Testing Program operated well during its second year. The nature of the substance abuse problem among clients supervised in the community was further revealed. The effectiveness of the Kentucky Substance Abuse Program in reducing recidivism was documented. There appears to be some distinction between the rate of positive testing for clients beginning supervision versus those who fit the standard testing profile. Testing of both segments of the population should be continued. However, something must be done with the cocaine-abusing offender. Apparently, both the sanctions and treatment provisions of the program cannot prevent continued abuse of cocaine.

Second, the extent of marijuana abused in this population is a serious problem which cannot be ignored. Marijuana is not a trivial drug. Marijuana smoking causes more severe lung damage than tobacco. Inciardi and McBride (1989, pp. 263–265) report that the respiratory burden in smoke particulates and absorption of carbon monoxide and tar from smoking just one joint is four times higher than from one cigarette. In addition, there is a "persistence of residue" effect since THC does not dissolve in water and becomes trapped, principally in the brain, lungs, liver, and reproductive organs. Also, the potency of marijuana has risen dramatically over the years. Marijuana is a major problem in Kentucky. In 1986, Kentucky reported that 76% of all 120 counties grew marijuana. In 1988, the State Police eradicated marijuana in all but nine Kentucky counties. In 1989, they detected 2980 plots, containing 438,588 plants.

Of course, the attraction of marijuana cultivation is its profitability. For example, Potter and Gaines (1990) state that a small, 60 square foot plot can yield about $60,000 worth of high-grade marijuana. The Kentucky Justice Cabinet (1990) estimates that, since 40 percent of the state marijuana crop was located and identified, potentially over 860,000 marijuana plants with an estimated value of up to 160 million dollars may be cultivated in Kentucky. A 30 day "Green/Gray Sweep" by the state police and the National Guard netted 151,132 plants with the help of helicopter surveillance (Lawson 1990). Governor Wallace G. Wilkinson has announced the formation of a new Marijuana Strike Force to coordinate the work of 13 state and federal agencies and destroy marijuana and prosecute those who grow it. The operation will be funded, in part, through a $3.9 million federal grant to the Kentucky National Guard to help law enforcement agencies with drug enforcement. The grant is the fifth largest among all states but the other four target the flow of drugs across the U.S. border.

This enforcement plan has already had an impact upon the marijuana supply. According to the drug testing program clients, the price of marijuana rose to meet and almost exceed that of cocaine.[6] Naturally, this higher price could lead the drug abusive client to turn to crime to support his/her habit. In this fashion, marijuana is as criminogenic a drug as cocaine and heroin. Its continued abuse by clients of community corrections should not be ignored.

REFERENCES

Belknap, J. (1987). "Routine Activity Theory and the Risk of Rape: Analyzing Ten Years of National Crime Survey Data." *Criminal Justice Policy Review* 2:337–356.

Blumstein, A., J. Cohen, J. A. Roth and C. A. Visher (eds.) (1986). *Criminal Careers and 'Career Criminals' Volumes I & II.* Washington, DC: National Academy Press.

Bocian, S. A. and C. W. Kempske (1990). "Inter-agency Evaluation, Diagnosis, and Referral Program." *APPA Perspectives, Special Issue, Substance Abuse: Strategies for Community Corrections Agencies* 14:34–35.

Bureau of Justice Statistics (1983a). *Prisoners and Alcohol.* Washington, DC: author.

—— (1983b). *Prisoners and Drugs.* Washington, DC: author.

Chaiken, M. R. and B. D. Johnson (1988). *Characteristics of Different Types of Drug-involved Offenders.* Washington, DC: National Institute of Justice.

Collins, J. J. (1986). "Relationship of Problem Drinking to Individual Offending Sequences." In A. Blumstein, J. Cohen, J. A. Roth and C. A. Visher (eds.), *Criminal Careers and 'Career Criminals', Volume II.* Washington, DC: National Institute of Justice.

Gendreau, P. and R. R. Ross (1987). "Revivification of Rehabilitation: Evidence from the 1980s." *Justice Quarterly* 4:349–408.

Graham, M. G. (1987). "Controlling Drug Abuse and Crime: A Research Update." *NIJ Reports.* Washington, DC: U.S. Department of Justice.

Gropper, B. A. (1985). *Probing the Link Between Drugs and Crime.* Washington, DC: National Institute of Justice.

Hadlock, N. (1990). "A.S.A.P.P.—A Substance Abuse Program for Probation." *APPA Perspectives, Special Issue, Substance Abuse: Strategies for Community Corrections Agencies* 14:46–49.

Hubbard, R. L., M. E. Marsden, J. V. Rachal, H. J. Harwood, E. R. Cavanaugh and H. M. Ginzburg (1989). *Drug Abuse Treatment: A National Study of Effectiveness.* Chapel Hill, NC: University of North Carolina Press.

Inciardi, J.A. (1986). *The War on Drugs.* Palo Alto, CA: Mayfield.

—— and D. C. McBride (1983). "Legalization: A High-risk Alternative in the War on Drugs." *American Behavioral Scientist* 32:259–289.

Innes, C. A. (1988). *Drug Use and Crime.* Washington, DC: Bureau of Justice Statistics.

Lawson, C. (1990). "Wilkinson Says State and U.S. Will Join to Fight Pot-growing." *The Courier Journal* July 17:B1,B3.

Leukefeld, C. G. (1990). "Opportunities for Strengthening Community Corrections with Coerced Drug Abuse Treatment." *APPA Perspectives, Special Issue, Substance Abuse: Strategies for Community Corrections Agencies* 14:6–9.

Levy, R. N. and J. E. Meyer (1990). "DIRECT Impact on Drug Offenders." *APPA Perspectives, Special Issue, Substance Abuse: Strategies for Community Correction Agencies* 14:28–31.

National Institute of Justice (1990). "Drugs and Crime." In L.J. Siegel (ed.), *American Justice Research of the National Institute of Justice.* Washington, DC: National Institute of Justice.

Nidorf, B. J., C. Arnold, J. Del Mastro, L. Duke, J. Etlinger, C. McClendon, J. Reeves and S. Yoder (1990). "A Specialized Approach to Drugs and Crime." *APPA Perspectives, Special Issue, Substance Abuse: Strategies For Community Correction Agencies* 14:32–33.

Norusis, M. J. (1990). *SPSS Advanced Statistics Student Guide.* Chicago, IL: SPSS, Inc.

Petersilia, J. and S. Turner (1990). "Comparing Intensive and Regular Supervision for High Risk Probationers: Early Results from an Experiment in California." *Crime and Delinquency* 36:33–51.

Potter, G. W. and L. K. Gaines (1990). "Organizing Crime in 'Copperhead County': An Ethnographic Look at Rural Crime Networks." Paper presented at the annual meeting of the Southern Sociological Association.

Robinson, J. J. and A. J. Lurigio (1990). "How About a Community Corrections Approach?" *APPA Perspectives, Special Issue, Substance Abuse: Strategies For Community Corrections Agencies* 14:22–27.

Vito, G. F. (1989a). "The Kentucky Substance Abuse Program: A Private Program to Treat Probationers and Parolees." *Federal Probation* 53: 65–72.

—— (1989b). "The War on Drugs—The Kentucky Substance Abuse Program." *Corrections Today* 51:34–37.

——, D. G. Wilson and T. J. Keil (1990). "Drug Testing, Treatment and Revocation: A Review of Program Findings." *Federal Probation* 54:37–43.

Weinman, B., V. Bowen and J. A. Mueller (1990). "Coordinated Interagency Drug Training and Technical Assistance Project." *APPA Perspectives, Special Issue, Substance Abuse: Strategies for Community Corrections Agencies* 14:51–53.

Wheeler, G.R. and A.S. Rudolph (1990). "Drug Testing and Recidivism of Houston Felony Probationers." *APPA Perspectives, Special Issue, Substance Abuse: Strategies For Community Corrections Agencies* 14:36–43.

Wish, E.D. and B.D. Johnson (1986). "Impact of Substance Abuse on Criminal Careers." In A. Blumstein, J. Cohen, J. A. Roth and C. A. Visher (eds.), *Criminal Careers and 'Career Criminals', Volume II.* Washington, DC: National Academy Press.

Wish, E. D. and J. A. O'Neil (1989). *Drug Use Forecasting, January to March 1989*. Washington DC: National Institute of Justice.

---

1 When comparisons were made between the two years of the program, only the "Old Cases" from the second year were used. This step was taken to insure accuracy since only "Old Cases" were tested during the first year.

2 Except for interval and ratio data, variables with more than two categories were reclassified. The most relevant variable was then omitted from the analysis as a reference category. For example, present offense was classified as violent, property, drug, and other. All categories were dichotomized and drug offense was kept out of the analysis.

3 During both years, equal numbers of blacks and whites were tested.

4 The DUF collects data in central booking facilities through voluntary and anonymous urine specimens and interviews with a sample of arrestees. Therefore, the samples are quite different than the clients under community supervision in the Louisville data (National Institute of Justice 1990).

5 The recidivism rates for each group were:

	Reincarceration	*Revocation*
Exits	17.4%	7.4%
Grads	0.9%	0.9%
Kontrols	0.6%	0.2%

6 In Jefferson County, the estimated street value of marijuana was $1,100 per pound and for cocaine was $80 to $100,000 per kilogram. Over 1400 pounds of marijuana and over 218 grams of cocaine were seized by Jefferson County local law enforcement agencies during fiscal year 1988.

3

The Academic Achievement of Juvenile Delinquents Relative to Intellectual Ability:
Implications for Research and Educational Program Development

Carol and Louis Veneziano

PREFACE

This research study was part of a larger project examining the characteristics of institutionalized juvenile delinquents, including academic, intellectual, personality, behavioral, and social variables. Its purpose was to establish sufficient information to develop better treatment programs for this population.

The study which follows was the result of the intellectual and academic assessment of adjudicated juvenile delinquents referred to a juvenile institution. The results indicated that the average scores on such measures for this group were considerably below that which would be expected on the average in the general population of adolescents in this age range. Generally, their average scores were one standard deviation below that of the general population, which is generally considered to be highly statistically significant. It is thus safe to say that these juvenile delinquents scored low on measures of IQ and academic achievement.

It is interesting to note, however, that group averages do not tell the entire story. There was actually considerable variability among the group of delinquents; some were more deficient than others. Furthermore, as this study illustrates, delinquents might score poorly in terms of academic achievement for different reasons. For some of these adolescents, poor academic achievement might be explained in terms of lower intellectual ability; for others, this explanation does not fit, as their academic achievement is below that which would be expected based on intellectual ability. Therefore, several explanations may be necessary in order to explain academic achievement among juvenile delinquents. Comparing group averages is often the beginning of studies that attempt to sort out various explanations that might be developed to explain those averages.

INTRODUCTION

It is generally believed, both empirically and anecdotally, that juvenile delinquents, as a group, are academic "underachievers." Furthermore, some authorities have even hypothesized that the failure of our school system to educate youths has given rise to an increase in the number who become delinquent (Maguin and Loeber 1996). Research has indicated that repeated delinquency is strongly linked with lower IQ, lower levels of academic achievement, and a higher incidence of learning disabilities. Despite the potential significance of such findings, the nature of the relationships among these variables has not been fully examined.

A substantial body of research indicates a consistent association between IQ scores and risk of official delinquency (Hirschi and Hindelang 1977). Numerous studies have found that the average IQ of delinquents is significantly lower than the average IQ of nondelinquents (Binder 1988; Glueck and Glueck 1950; Kelly 1971). Some studies report a difference as low as 8 points (Quay 1987), while other studies report a difference as large as 20 points (Yeudall, Fromm-Auch, and Davies 1982).

Most studies report a difference of approximately 15 points (Binder 1988). Since, by definition and convention, the mean IQ of the general population is 100 with a standard deviation of 15 points, this indicates that the mean IQ of delinquents, 85, is one standard deviation unit below the mean IQ of the general population. Further, while the mean IQ of the general population falls within the Average range (90 to 109), the mean IQ of juvenile delinquents falls within the Low Average range (80 to 89). Other studies have indicated that only very small percentages of delinquents would be considered above average (Bachman 1970), while slightly more than 25% of the general population would fall in the High Average (110 to 119), Superior (120 to 129), and Very Superior (130 and above) ranges.

The argument has been made that the link between IQ scores and delinquency is spurious; that is, less intelligent youths may be more likely to be processed through the juvenile justice system. The relationship, however, not only holds for official delinquency, but also for self-reported delinquency (Wolfgang, Figlio, and Sellin 1972; West and Farrington 1973). Thus, the association cannot be entirely explained on the basis of selective labeling and processing. Moreover, the relationship cannot be explained entirely on the basis of social class or race, although there are IQ differences among racial and social class groups (Lynam, Moffitt, and Stouthamer-Loeber 1993). When groups are stratified by race and social class, the association still remains between lower IQ scores, particularly verbal scores, and delinquency (Tracy, Wolfgang, and Figlio 1990; Maguin and Loeber 1996).

Lower levels of educational achievement have also been associated with delinquency in many studies. Official delinquents have generally been found to be more than two grade levels below what would be expected on the basis of age, with most of the studies focusing on reading achievement (Silberberg and Silberberg 1971; Gottfredson 1981; Hawkins and Lishner 1987; Williams and

McGee 1994). In addition, longitudinal studies have reported consistent associations between lower educational attainment and self-reported aggression and delinquency, even after controlling for family and social class variables (White, Pandina, and LaGrange 1987). Delinquency has also been associated with school failure, behavioral problems in school and dropping out (Patterson and Dishion 1985; White, Pandina, and LaGrange 1987; Denno 1990; Walker et al. 1993).

It could be argued that research investigating the relationship between academic achievement and delinquency has been plagued by two major problems. The first is that, given the substantial body of research concerning lower levels of measured intelligence among juvenile delinquents, academic achievement must be viewed in relation to IQ. That is, because of the strong relationship between IQ and academic achievement, is the academic achievement of delinquents commensurate with their lower levels of measured intelligence or not? It is unrealistic to assume that an individual with an IQ of 80 would be performing at the same level academically as an individual with an IQ of 100, even though both individuals may be in the same grade.

The second problem is related to the first, and it involves making meaningful comparisons of academic achievement relative to intellectual ability by using a comparable scale of measurement, such as deviation IQs. Grade equivalent scores have generally been used as the measure of academic achievement, and these scores are at an ordinal level of measurement. Grade equivalent scores are developed by administering a test to representative samples of children over a range of consecutive grade levels. Next, the mean score for children at each grade level is computed. Because the school year is typically ten months long (September to June), fractions in the mean are expressed as decimals by linear interpolation (Cohen, Swerdlik, and Phillips 1996).

For example, an individual in the sixth grade receives a grade equivalent score of 12.2 on a mathematics test. Does that really mean that this child is capable of doing twelfth-grade math? Probably not, in that it is highly unlikely that he/she would have even been exposed to twelfth-grade mathematical concepts yet. What his/her score means is that he/she correctly answered the same number of questions on a test of sixth-grade mathematics as beginning twelfth-grade students. Clearly, this individual is above average in terms of knowledge of sixth-grade mathematics, but how far above average is impossible to say. At best, grade equivalent scores represent an ordinal level of measurement.

A further correlate of delinquency relevant to educational achievement is that of learning disabilities. In an early review of the literature, Murray (1976) found that a number of studies provided evidence for a link between delinquency and learning disabilities, despite methodological problems. Since that time, follow-up studies of children with learning disabilities and attention deficit disorder have consistently found higher levels of delinquency and academic problems in these children compared with controls (Spreen 1981; Satterfield, Hoppe, and Schell 1982; McGee and Share 1988; Mannuzza, Gittelmann-Klein, and Giampino 1989; Moffitt 1990).

In summary, a substantial body of research has indicated that low IQ, low levels of academic achievement, and learning disabilities are correlates of delinquency. Such studies, however, have not directly examined academic achievement relative to IQ scores among delinquents. Furthermore, grade equivalents have generally been used to define academic achievement, and because these scores are measured on an ordinal scale, the conclusions that can be drawn on the basis of such measures are limited. The present study was designed to directly compare IQ scores with academic achievement scores using deviation IQs, which provide a comparable scale of measurement for both academic achievement and intellectual ability.

METHOD

Subjects

The subjects were 411 institutionalized adolescent males aged 12 to 15 who were committed as adjudicated delinquents to a state department of corrections. Every male committed during a one-year period of time who completed the classification process was included in the sample. The only exclusions were those transferred to another facility or released by the court before they completed the five workday classification process. During this period of time, 452 students were admitted, with 411 or 90.9% completing the classification process.

The subjects ranged in age from 11 years 7 months to 16 years 4 months, with a mean age of 14 years 9 months. Fifty-two percent were white and 49% were African-American. The sample consisted of 3.6% status offenders, while the remaining 96.4% were classified as delinquent offenders. Slightly less than half (46%) of the sample were committed from the largest urban area in the state, 67.6% were serving their first commitment, and 57.9% were committed for one offense. About two-thirds were committed for property offenses; the second most common offense was violation of probation.

Procedure

Every juvenile admitted to the facility where this research was conducted was placed in a "classification class" in which they remained for the first five working days of their commitment. While they were in the classification class, each student was assessed in eight developmental areas, including a comprehensive Academic/Intellectual assessment.

Tests Administered

The components of the academic/intellectual assessment included the Culture Fair Intelligence Test (CFIT), the Peabody Picture Vocabulary Test-Revised (PPVT-R), the California Achievement Test (CAT), and the Wide Range Achievement Test (WRAT). In order to make meaningful comparisons between different individuals taking these and similar tests, test developers routinely use a variety of standard scores.

Standard scores are scores that have a specified mean and a specified standard deviation, which provide a meaningful description of the exact location of an individual's score within the distribution of scores generated by the normative population (Gravetter and Wallnau 1996). In the brief description of each of the tests that follows, the mean and standard deviation of each type of standard score will be provided.

The CFIT is a nonverbal group intelligence test that yields a deviation IQ (mean = 100, standard deviation = 15). The PPVT-R is a measure of receptive language and proficiency with standard American English, and it yields two scores: a standard score (mean = 100, standard deviation = 15) and an age equivalent score. The WRAT is an academic achievement screening test, yielding grade equivalent and standard scores (mean = 100, standard deviation = 15) in the areas of reading, spelling, and arithmetic.

The CAT is a standardized achievement battery, assessing achievement in the areas of reading vocabulary, reading comprehension, spelling, language mechanics, language expression, mathematics computation, mathematics concepts and applications, and reference skills. Subtests can be combined to obtain total reading, language, mathematics, and battery composite scores. The CAT yields a number of derived scores, including grade equivalent and scale scores (mean = 600, standard deviation = 100).

Data Analysis

To examine the relationship between academic achievement and intellectual ability, the data were analyzed using descriptive statistics that directly compared CFIT deviation IQs with the CAT scale scores and the WRAT standard scores. Since the CFIT and WRAT generated derived scores with the same mean (100) and standard deviation (15), they could be directly compared. Because the scale scores on the CAT had a different mean (600) and standard deviation (100), it was necessary to linearly transform them into a set of scores that also had a mean of 100 and a standard deviation of 15.

The linear transformation employed was quite simple, and it is important to note that a linear transformation does not alter the shape of the original distribution of scores, nor does it change the location of any individual's score in the distribution (Gravetter and Wallnau 1996). Linear transformations provide a mechanism for transforming scores with different means and standard deviations to the same type of standard score so that direct comparisons can be easily made.

Using the techniques of linear transformation discussed by Roscoe (1975), the CAT scale scores were converted to standard scores using the following formula:

$$DIQ = \left\{ \left[(ScSc - 600)/100 \right] * 15 \right\} + 100$$

where

DIQ: Deviation IQ

ScSc: Scale score to be converted

600: Mean of scale score distribution

100: Standard deviation of scale score distribution

15: Standard deviation of deviation IQ distribution

100: Mean of deviation IQ distribution

In this manner, every student's scale scores on the CAT were converted to deviation IQs.

Each subject's CFIT IQ score was then subtracted from the deviation IQ scores for each of the subscales on the WRAT, as well as from each of the deviation IQ scores of the subtests on the CAT, and the resulting difference scores were then placed into one of seven categories, based on CFIT IQ scores. The categories were based on the generally accepted premise that differences between measures greater than one standard deviation (i.e., 15 points) are statistically significant (Cohen, Swerdlik, and Phillips 1996). The other categories were developed by establishing ad hoc ranges around intellectual ability in increments of 5 points. The labels attached to these categories were based on the assumption that academic achievement, as measured by deviation IQs (DIQ), should be highly correlated with intellectual ability (i.e., an individual with an IQ of 90 should have DIQ scores close to 90 on measures of academic achievement).

These categories were as follows:

1. Academic DIQ score minus CFIT IQ score > 14;
   Very much above expected academic achievement level, based on IQ score.

2. 9 < academic DIQ score minus CFIT IQ score < 15;
   Much above expected level.

3. 5 < academic DIQ score minus CFIT IQ score < 10;
   Above expected level.

4. −6 < academic DIQ score minus CFIT IQ score < 6;
   At expected academic achievement level.

5. −10 < academic DIQ score minus CFIT IQ score < −5;
   Near expected academic achievement level.

6. −15 < academic DIQ score minus CFIT IQ score < −9;
   Below expected level.

7. Academic DIQ score minus CFIT IQ score < −14;
   Much below, possible learning disability or other problem.

Results

A summary of the results for the CFIT, the PPVT-R, and the WRAT are given in Table 3.1. The mean CFIT was 87 for the sample, and the mean PPVT-R was 72.1, with an age equivalent score of 11.0. On the WRAT, grade equivalent scores were 5.4, 4.6, and 5.4 for reading, spelling, and arithmetic respectively, with corresponding DIQ scores of 80.4, 77.7, and 75.0.

The results for the CAT for the sample are presented separately in Table 3.2. The mean DIQ scores for the subtests on the CAT ranged from 79 to 85. The mean DIQ score for total reading

Table 3-1   Academic/Intellectual Test Results for the CFIT, the PPVT-R, and the WRAT.

Culture Fair Intelligence Test	
Mean	87.0
S.D.	14.5
Peabody Picture Vocabulary Test–Revised	
Standard Score	
Mean	72.1
S.D.	14.5
Age Equivalent Score	
Mean	11.0
S.D.	5.3
Wide Range Achievement Test	

	Reading
Grade Equivalent	
Mean	5.4
S.D.	1.9
Standard Score	
Mean	80.4
S.D.	14.7

	Spelling
Grade Equivalent	
Mean	4.6
S.D.	1.7
Standard Score	
Mean	77.7
S.D.	11.3

	Arithmetic
Grade Equivalent	
Mean	5.4
S.D.	1.3
Standard Score	
Mean	75
S.D.	7.9

was 79.7; for total language, 83.4; for total mathematics, 79.9; and for total battery, 79.8. Mean grade equivalents for the subtests ranged from 5.7 to 6.3; in other words, academic achievement

Table 3–2 Summary Table of Standard Score and Grade Equivalents for the California Achievement Test.

Subtest

Reading Vocabulary		
Standard Score	Mean	79.9
	S.D.	10.0
Grade Equivalent	Mean	5.7
	S.D.	2.4
Reading Comprehension		
Standard Score	Mean	81.5
	S.D.	11.4
Grade Equivalent	Mean	5.8
	S.D.	2.7
Total Reading		
Standard Score	Mean	79.7
	S.D.	11.0
Grade Equivalent	Mean	5.8
	S.D.	2.4
Spelling		
Standard Score	Mean	85.2
	S.D.	11.5
Grade Equivalent	Mean	6.1
	S.D.	3.0
Language Mechanics		
Standard Score	Mean	85.4
	S.D.	9.8
Grade Equivalent	Mean	5.6
	S.D.	2.8
Language Expression		
Standard Score	Mean	84.1
	S.D.	9.5
Grade Equivalent	Mean	5.7
	S.D.	2.7
Total Language		
Standard Score	Mean	83.4
	S.D.	9.8
Grade Equivalent	Mean	5.6
	S.D.	2.5
Mathematics Computation		
Standard Score	Mean	80.8
	S.D.	10.5
Grade Equivalent	Mean	6.3
	S.D.	2.0

Table 3–2 (*continued*)

Subtest		
Mathematics Concepts and Applications		
Standard Score	Mean	79.4
	S.D.	9.6
Grade Equivalent	Mean	5.6
	S.D.	2.2
Total Mathematics		
Standard Score	Mean	79.9
	S.D.	9.4
Grade Equivalent	Mean	6.9
	S.D.	2.0
Reference Skills		
Standard Score	Mean	82.1
	S.D.	10.3
Grade Equivalent	Mean	5.6
	S.D.	2.6
Total Battery		
Standard Score	Mean	79.8
	S.D.	9.9
Grade Equivalent	Mean	5.7
	S.D.	2.0

scores on the CAT were indicative of fifth- to sixth-grade level achievement.

As was described previously, the academic achievement scores on the CAT were classified for each of the subtests in one of seven categories, indicating whether each subject was above, at, or below their achievement level based on their intellectual ability as measured on the CFIT. Table 3.3 presents the percentages of the sample falling into each of the seven categories. As can be seen from this table, 25 to 35% of the sample fell at their expected grade level. For total scores, from Table 3.3, the following results can be noted: for the total reading score, 49.4% of the sample were near, at, or above expected level of academic achievement, with the other half below or significantly below expected achievement level; and for total battery scores, 49.5% were near, at, or above the expected achievement level, based on CFIT IQ.

Table 3–3 Academic Acheivement Classifications on the California Achievement Test Based on the Intellectual Ability Level Established by the Culture Fair Intelligence Test.

	Percentages						
Category:	Very Much Above	Much Above	Above	At	Near	Below	LD?
Reading Vocabulary	1.9	3.5	4.6	26.4	14.6	18.3	30.7
Reading Comprehension	4.0	4.3	6.2	27.2	12.7	16.7	28.8
Total Reading	1.6	3.5	5.7	25.9	12.7	17.0	33.7
Spelling	8.9	9.2	7.0	29.1	14.3	10.5	21.0
Language Mechanics	5.1	8.4	7.8	35.3	13.5	13.7	16.2
Language Expression	4.3	4.6	8.6	35.6	11.9	16.2	18.9
Total Language	3.0	4.3	8.4	34.0	15.4	15.9	19.1
Mathematics Computation	2.7	4.9	5.7	30.2	12.1	11.6	32.9
Mathematics Concepts	2.2	2.4	3.8	24.0	16.4	19.1	32.1
Total Mathematics	1.9	3.5	3.5	29.6	12.4	18.3	30.7
Reference Skills	3.2	4.6	6.2	29.4	18.1	14.6	24.0
Total Battery	1.1	3.2	3.5	28.0	13.7	18.3	32.1

The results for the WRAT are provided in Table 3.4. For the reading subtest, 62.5% fell near, at, or above the expected level of achievement based on IQ, whereas 65% and 70% fell near, at, or above the expected academic achievement level for the spelling and arithmetic subtests, respectively.

DISCUSSION

The sample scored lower on measures of intelligence and academic achievement than would be expected in the general

Table 3-4 Academic Achievement Classifications on the Wide Range Achievement Test Based on the Intellectual Ability Level Established by the Culture Fair Intelligence Test.

| | Percentages | | |
Category	Reading	Spelling	Arithmetic
Very Much Above	0.0	0.0	2.5
Much Above	2.5	0.0	15.0
Above	7.5	40.0	22.5
At	45.0	15.0	22.5
Near	7.5	10.0	7.5
Below	7.5	7.5	15.0
Possible LD	30.0	27.5	15.0

population. On a nonverbal test of intelligence, the average IQ was 87, which falls in the Low Average range (80 to 89). This means that half of the delinquents scored below 87, as compared to only 19% in the general population scoring below 87. The verbal intelligence of these delinquents, as measured by the PPVT-R, was even lower, with a mean score of 72, which falls in the Borderline range (70 to 79). This means that half of the delinquents scored below 72, as compared to only 3% in the general population scoring below 72. With respect to mastery of standard American English, these adolescents were, on the average, 3.5 to 4 years below what would be expected, and thus were deficient in verbal skills.

Furthermore, this sample scored, on the average, below grade level on measures of academic achievement. The vast majority of students in this sample (about 85%) were in the seventh, eighth, or ninth grade in the public schools, but on the WRAT and the CAT they scored on the average at the fifth grade level—at least two grade levels below what would be expected on the basis of chronological age and placement according to public school grade.

Academic achievement relative to intellectual ability was compared using DIQ scores, a considerably better scale in terms of drawing inferences than grade equivalents. DIQ scores on the CAT ranged from 79 to 85, while the average CFIT IQ was 87, not much higher than the mean DIQ scores on the CAT. On the average, therefore, academic achievement DIQ scores were similar to intellectual ability DIQ scores.

When the subjects were classified according to whether they were above, at, or below expected academic achievement level based on CFIT IQ, the results indicated that at least half of the delinquents, and higher percentages in some areas of achievement, were functioning in terms of academic achievement at their expected level based on a measure of intelligence. At least half of the sample were therefore not found to be underachievers. On the other hand, one-third to one-half of the delinquents were at academic achievement levels below what would be expected based on IQ.

It would thus appear that these delinquents are not homogeneous as a group in terms of academic achievement. Although the subjects in this sample were almost always below their expected level of achievement in terms of their chronological ages, about half of them were doing about as well as could be expected. Considering the fact that many of these delinquents probably have numerous social, behavioral, and family difficulties, it can be argued that their academic attainment is actually reasonable, relative to their circumstances and ability. If average grade equivalent scores are compared only to public school grades, the academic achievement of the delinquents would seem poor. However, the results of this study indicate that a substantial number of the delinquents do not perform as well as many adolescents their age, but because their intellectual abilities are lower on the average than for people in the general population, it would be expected that their academic achievement levels would also be below average.

On the other hand, nearly half of the sample did have levels of academic achievement that were below what would be expected relative to intellectual ability. However, this portion of the sample appeared to consist of two different subgroups, possible underachievers and possible learning disabled individuals. In the study,

10 to 19% (depending on the subtest) scored below what would be expected relative to ability (see Tables 3.3 and 3.4), while an additional 16 to 34% scored low enough to meet the criteria for a learning disability. Contrary to popular opinion, delinquents who are genuine underachievers did not constitute a large percentage of the sample.

The results also demonstrate that substantial portions of the sample scored significantly below their expected level of academic achievement relative to intellectual ability, pointing to learning disabilities or other problems. One-third of the delinquents were significantly below their expected ability in reading, mathematics, and total battery scores. Thus, while a slight majority of the delinquents had educational attainment commensurate with intellectual ability, a substantial minority were significantly below expected achievement levels.

The reasons for the low levels of academic achievement among one-third of the delinquents need to be explored in future research. As the findings suggest, possible learning disabilities (LD) could be involved, as LD typically is operationally defined in terms of academic achievement being significantly below intellectual ability. Recent studies have suggested that one-third of delinquent samples are learning disabled. However, other possibilities cannot be ruled out, including mental retardation, physical handicaps (e.g., visual, auditory, or motor), emotional disturbance, inappropriate or insufficient teaching, and severe environmental/cultural disadvantage.

The results of this study have important research implications, as they demonstrate that the academic deficits of delinquents have multiple causes. For a majority of the sample, low levels of educational achievement would appear to reflect only intellectual ability, rather than underachievement or learning disability, whereas for some of these students, alternative explanations other than ability need to be sought. If academic deficits among juvenile delinquents have multiple causes, it seems likely that no one explanation can account for the associations among intelligence, academic achievement, LD, and juvenile delinquency. Rather, any explanation might be expected to apply to subsets of juvenile delinquents.

The results from the present study also have implications for educational treatment programs. Institutionalized adolescents are highly likely to require considerable remedial work. The results clearly indicate that, as a group, delinquents, on the average, have academic deficiencies in all areas of achievement when compared to adolescents in the general population. In particular, these young offenders were seriously lacking in language proficiency. Although there is undoubtedly a strong cultural and class bias in such a measure, the fact still remains that language mastery is an important skill in American society, and an area in which these delinquents demonstrate a significant deficit.

Given these serious academic deficiencies, it seems likely that delinquents' school experiences have been aversive, and perhaps for some, damaging to self-confidence and self-esteem. About half of the delinquents in the sample lack the intellectual ability to do well in school and to perform at the expected public school grade. They probably encounter a number of problems in school on a daily basis, as they are unable to meet the expectations placed on them. This study also indicates that there is a substantial group who are deficient in academic attainment, below that which they should be capable of achieving. Their low levels of academic achievement could also cause them difficulty. In developing programs for delinquents, it would be important to keep such considerations in mind.

In terms of developing academic programs for institutionalized offenders, the results suggest that programs should emphasize a standard curriculum for those youths whose achievement is reasonably commensurate with ability, but that it would be important to place students in such a curriculum based on their intellectual abilities, not on their actual or expected grade placements. That is, a fourteen-year-old eighth-grade student (who should probably actually be in the ninth grade) of low average or borderline intelligence functioning at the fifth-grade level is capable of satisfactorily handling a standard fifth-grade curriculum and progressing from this point. Those students not profiting from standard instruction, who are deficient in academic achievement relative to ability, need to be further evaluated and considered for special education or alternative educational programs. Further, the results of the academic achievement and intellectual ability tests suggest that emphasis should be placed on language enrichment designed to increase an individual's hearing and sight vocabulary, as well as focusing on mastering mathematical computations.

Finally, the diversity found among the delinquents indicates that it would be inappropriate to assume that institutionalized delinquents as a group are simply underachievers who need to be motivated, or that they are learning disabled, or indeed that they fit into any one particular category. Rather, it would seem that many of these students will have a variety of educational difficulties, and that institutional programs will have to carefully evaluate students and be prepared to utilize a variety of individualized educational approaches if they are to be maximally effective. Given the well-documented nature of the academic problems of juvenile delinquents, it would seem that institutional educational programs could have an important and positive impact on this group.

In summary, in the lay community and among workers in the juvenile justice system, it is generally held that juvenile delinquents are underachievers. The present study indicates that the majority of juvenile delinquents are not underachievers, and that there are probably a number of reasons that account for low levels of academic attainment. Comparisons of academic achievement and intellectual ability in the past have generally utilized grade equivalent scores and thus have not been particularly meaningful, a problem the present study attempted to remedy. Based on the findings, intellectual ability would seem to be the single most important factor for many incarcerated delinquents in explaining low academic achievement, and therefore needs to be considered in planning a curriculum in juvenile institutions. The dynamics for students who do not achieve relative to ability would appear to be an interesting area for further research.

REFERENCES

Bachman, J. G. 1970. *Youth in transition.* The Impact of Family Background and Intelligence on Tenth-Grade Boys, vol. 2. Ann Arbor: University of Michigan, Institute for Social Research.

Binder, A. 1988. Juvenile delinquency. *Annual Review of Psychology* 39: 253–82.

Cohen, R. J., M. E. Swerdlik, and S. M. Phillips. 1996. *Psychological testing and assessment: An introduction to tests and measurements.* 3rd ed. Mountain View, CA: Mayfield.

Denno, D. 1990. *Biology and violence: From birth to adulthood.* New York: Cambridge University Press.

Glueck, S., and E. Glueck. 1950. *Unraveling juvenile delinquency.* New York: Commonwealth Fund.

Gottfredson, G. D. 1981. Schooling and Delinquency. In *New directions in the rehabilitation of criminal offenders,* edited by S. E. Martin, L. B. Sechrest, and R. Redner. Washington, D.C.: National Academy Press.

Gravetter, F. J., and L. B. Wallnau. 1996. Statistics for the behavioral sciences: A first course for students of psychology and education. 4th ed. Minneapolis: West Publishing.

Hawkins, J. D., and D. M. Lishner. 1987. Schooling and Delinquency. In *Handbook on Crime and Delinquency Prevention,* edited by E. H. Johnson. New York: Greenwood.

Hirschi, T., and M. J. Hindelang. 1977. Intelligence and delinquency: A revisionist review. *American Sociological Review* 42:571–87.

Kelly, D. H. 1971. School failure, academic self-evaluation, and school avoidance and deviant behavior. *Youth and Society* 2:489–502.

Lynam, D., T. E. Moffitt, and M. Stouthamer-Loeber. 1993. Explaining the relation between IQ and delinquency: Class, race, test motivation, school failure, or self-control? *Journal of Abnormal Psychology* 102:187–96.

Maguin, E., and R. Loeber. 1996. Academic performance and delinquency. In *Crime and justice: A review of research*, edited by M. Tonry. Chicago: University of Chicago Press.

Mannuzza, S., R. Gittelmann-Klein, P. H. Konig, and T. L. Giampino. 1989. Hyperactive boys almost grown up. *Archives of General Psychiatry* 46:1073–79.

McGee, R., and D. Share. 1988. Attention Deficit Disorder-Hyperactivity and academic failure: Which comes first and what should be treated. *Journal of the American Academy of Child and Adolescent Psychiatry* 27:318–25.

Moffitt, T. E. 1990. The neuropsychology of juvenile delinquency: A critical review. In *Crime and Justice: A Review of Research*, vol. 12, edited by M. Tonry and N. Morris. Chicago: University of Chicago Press.

Murray, C. 1976. A study of dyslexia and delinquency. *Academic Therapy Quarterly* 4: 177–87.

Patterson, G. R., and T. J. Dishion. 1985. Contributions of families and peers to delinquency. *Criminology* 23:63–79.

Quay, H. C. 1987. Intelligence. In *Handbook of juvenile delinquency*, edited by H. C. Quay. New York: Wiley.

Roscoe, J. 1975. *Fundamental research statistics for the behavioral sciences.* New York: Holt, Rinehart, and Winston.

Satterfield, J. H., C. M. Hoppe, and A. M. Schell. 1982. A prospective study of delinquency in 110 adolescent boys with attention disorder and 88 normal adolescent boys. *American Journal of Psychiatry* 139:795–98.

Silberberg, N. E., and M. C. Silberberg. 1971. School achievement and delinquency. *Review of Educational Research* 41:17–33.

Spreen, O. 1981. The relationship between learning disability, neurological impairment, and delinquency. *Journal of Nervous and Mental Disease* 169:791–99.

Tracy, P. E., M. E. Wolfgang, and R. M. Figlio. 1990. *Delinquency careers in two birth cohorts.* New York: Plenum.

Walker, H. M., S. Stieber, E. Ramsey, and R. E. O'Neill. 1993. Fifth grade school adjustment and later arrest rate: A longitudinal study of middle school antisocial boys. *Journal of Child and Family Studies* 2:295–315.

West, D. J., and D. P. Farrington. 1973. *Who becomes delinquent?* London: Heinemann.

White, H. R., R. J. Pandina, and R. L. LaGrange. 1987. Longitudinal predictors of serious substance use and delinquency. *Criminology* 25:715–40.

Williams, S., and R. McGee. 1994. Reading attainment and juvenile delinquency. *Journal of Child Psychology and Psychiatry* 35:441–59.

Wolfgang, M. E., R. M. Figlio, and T. Sellin. 1972. *Delinquency in a birth cohort.* Chicago: University of Chicago Press.

Yeudall, L., D. Fromm-Auch, and P. Davies. 1982. Neuropsychological impairment of persistent delinquency. *Journal of Nervous and Mental Diseases* 170:257–65.

4

Identifying Employment Criteria and Requisite Skills for the Position of Police Chief:
Preliminary Findings*

M. L. Dantzker

PREFACE

The purpose of this research was to begin examining what police chiefs perceived as necessary criteria and skills for those individuals seeking to become police chiefs. The information was gathered through a questionnaire sent to 115 police chiefs. Considering that the data was primarily nominal and ordinal in nature, it was believed that the best way to report it was using measures of central tendency: frequencies, percentages, ranges, mean, mode, and median.

---

* Reprinted with permission of the Academy of Criminal Justice Sciences. Orginally published as: M. L. Dantzker. 1994. "Identifying Employment Criteria and Requisite Skills for the Position of Police Chief: Preliminary Findings," *Police Forum* 4(3):9–12.

INTRODUCTION

One of the challenges for modern-day law enforcement has been to improve the quality of sworn personnel through extensive training and higher education. Entry requirements for police officers have long been a subject of concern, debate, and change among practitioners, academicians, citizens, and commissions. The body of research and literature advocating higher hiring standards continues to grow steadily. The level of training and education among police officers is increasing (Carter & Sapp 1990). This growth and change provide additional challenges to law enforcement. One such challenge that, to date, appears to have received little attention is the issue of improved police leadership. It seems that while we continue to improve the quality of police officers entering law enforcement, little has been done with respect to the individual who must offer leadership and management to these new officers.

As early as 1920, when Ray Fosdick released his study of police leadership, which emphasized how mediocre police leadership was in this country, the quality of police leadership has been an issue that has received limited scrutiny (See Cox 1990; Goldstein 1977; Lynch 1975; Witham 1985). Hunt and Margenau (1993) note that little is known about police chiefs primarily because very little quantitative or qualitative information exists that describes the police chief role. This is an extremely interesting phenomenon when one considers the importance of the role of the police chief.

Witham (1986) contends that, "police executives are the most critical group related to improving law enforcement. Police organizations are unlikely to be better than their leaders" (p. 45). Furthermore, "It is widely recognized that the most critical ingredient in the success of an organization is the quality of its leadership. Although police leaders cannot single-handedly upgrade law enforcement, there is no single group as important to the process" (Witham, 1987:6). Although limited, the literature tends to support this belief (See Chandler 1982; Enter 1986a; Goldstein 1977; Masini & Playfair 1978; Maniha 1973; Witham 1985). Yet, despite the recognition of the importance of this individual, policing research has paid little attention to who or how qualified this person is. One might think that police leadership and management have been completely ignored; yet, this is not true. Criminal justice programs have long offered courses on police administration, organization, and management. Several textbooks are available that identify what skills a police executive should possess and how to use those skills (see Gaines Southerland & Angell 1991; Swanson Territo, & Taylor 1993; Wilson & McLaren 1977). Finally, in recent years, to further assist in the development of police managers several schools and institutes have emerged that specialize in management training (e.g., Southwestern Law Enforcement Institute, the Institute of Police Management and Technology, and the Southern Police Institute), as well as courses offered through the FBI. However, despite the increased availability of management training, a minimum amount of consideration has been given as to the employment requirements for the hiring of the potential police chief. Historically, many police chiefs work their way up through the ranks (Chandler 1982; Crank 1987; Enter 1986b). In many instances this progression provides an extremely limited amount of training and preparation for the position of police chief, resulting in inadequately prepared leaders (see Lynch 1975; Witham, 1985, 1986, 1987).

As noted by Cox (1990),

> The quality of leadership in police organizations has varied tremendously. Some police organizations currently carefully select entry personnel, carefully evaluate their potential for promotion, promote based on merit, and prepare those who are promoted by sending them to appropriate training and/or educational programs. Others do none of these things (p. 175).

Whether hired from within or outside the police agency, it has been advocated that the requirements for the position of police chief should be relatively consistent and should include criteria that best suits the position (see Cox 1990; Goldstein 1977; Hunt & Magenau 1993; Maniha 1973; Witham 1986). Yet, this is where the problem begins. What are the criteria for the position of police chief? What skills should a candidate possess? It is answers to these questions that are sorely lacking in current literature. Granted, police administration textbooks may offer theoretically-based answers, but the application of these theories often receive little support from the practical arena. Research offers little support. Therefore, an effort to increase the research of requirements for the position of police chief is underway. This article reports early findings based on a survey of a purposive sample of police chiefs.

METHODOLOGY

The objective of the continuing research is to try to identify the qualifications criteria for the position of police chief. To begin work toward this objective a two-phase methodology was used. Phase one was the content analyses of advertisements for the position of police chief. (The results of this phase will be reported elsewhere). Phase two included a survey of a purposive sample of police chiefs and the analyses of the data collected. (Phase three will consist of surveying a larger random sample of police chiefs currently underway.)

Phase two involved designing and mailing a questionnaire (See Appendix) to a purposive sample of police chiefs. The questionnaire consisted of three sections: agency demographics, personal demographics, and police chief qualifications. Agency demographics consisted of department size (sworn and non-sworn), jurisdiction population, budget, education requirements for recruits, and education requirements for promotion. Personal demographics as applied to chiefs included years of law enforcement experience, years as police chief of current department (which also included whether hired from inside or outside and related questions), rank before becoming a police chief, years of police management experience before becoming a police chief, and general demographics such as age, gender, ethnicity, education.

The section on police chief qualifications required respondents to rank order by importance (1–12, 1 being most important) twelve skills identified through a review of police administration literature as necessary for a police chief (For example see Gaines et al., 1991; Swanson et al. 1993; Wilson & Mclaren 1977).

Next, respondents were asked to rank order (1–10) items found as requirements for potential police chiefs from the advertisements. In addition to the two ranking sections, respondents were provided an open-ended question about qualifications for potential police chiefs and whether a police chief should be hired from inside or outside the department and why.

The validity of the questionnaire was supported through face validity (based on researcher's experience, review of the literature, analysis of the advertisements, and review by a police chief). Reliability was accepted because it appeared to measure what it was designed to measure.

The questionnaire was sent to 115 police chiefs in Cook County, Illinois, with a stamped, self-addressed envelope. Fifty-eight (50.4%) usable questionnaires were returned.

RESULTS

Beginning with agency demographics, agency sizes (sworn personnel) ranged from 8 to 125 with a mean of 42.5. The largest percentage of agencies (n = 40, 69%) had a sworn staff of under 50. The range for non-sworn personnel was 0 to 70 with a mean of 15.6. Twenty-two (37.9%) had non-sworn staffs of under 10. The population of the agency's jurisdiction was divided into four categories with the largest number of agencies, 27 (46.6%), indicating serving populations between 10,001 and 25,000. Budget was also divided into four categories with a majority of agencies reporting a budget between 1 and 5 million (n = 41, 70.7%). As for educational requirements for recruits, 48 (82.8%) require a high school diploma, while 51 (87.9%) have no further educational requirements for promotion (see Table 4.1).

Regarding personal demographics of chiefs, the range for law enforcement experience was 16 to 41 years with a mean of 25.5 years of enforcement experience (under 25 years and over 25

Table 4–1 Agency Demographics (Sample, n = 58).

Variable	Frequency	Percentage
Department Size (Sworn)		
Under 50	40	69.0%
51–75	10	17.2
Over 75	7	12.1
Missing	1	1.7
Department Size (Non-sworn)		
Under 10	22	37.9
11–20	18	31.0
Over 21	16	27.6
Missing	2	3.4
Jurisdiction Population		
Under 10,000	12	20.7
10,001–25,000	27	46.6
25,001–50,000	13	22.4
50,001–100,000	5	8.6
Missing	1	1.7
Budget		
Under $1 million	5	8.6
1–5 million	41	71.7
6–10 million	5	8.6
Over 10 million	1	1.7
Missing	6	10.3
Educational Requirement (for recruits)		
High School diploma	48	82.8
Associates degree	5	8.6
Bachelors degree	2	3.4
No degree, but college hours		
under 30 hours	1	1.7
30–60 hours	1	1.7
60–90 hours	1	1.7
Educational Requirement (for promotion)		
None	51	87.9
Associates degree	2	3.4
Bachelors degree	3	5.2
Other	2	3.4

Table 4-2 Personal Demographics, Sample Respondents (N = 58).

Variable	Frequency	Percentage
Years of Police Experience		
Under 25	29	50.0%
Over 25	29	50.0
Years as Current Police Chief		
Under 6	36	62.1
Over 6	22	37.9
Hired		
From within	38	65.5
From outside	19	32.8
Rank (before becoming a PC for the first time)		
Sergeant	5	8.6
Lieutenant	13	22.4
Captain	12	20.7
Deputy Chief	23	39.7
Other	5	8.6
Education		
High school diploma	8	13.8
Associates degree	12	20.7
Bachelors degree	11	19.0
Masters degree	24	41.4

years was evenly divided at 29 respondents each). Years as current police chief ranged from 1 to 26 years with a mean of 6.2 (36 had been chief for under 6 years). Thirty-eight (65.5%) had been hired from within. Of the 19 chiefs who had been hired from outside the department, 11 (57.9%) had been police chiefs elsewhere; the other 8 had been between the ranks of sergeant and deputy chief. The years as police chief ranged from 3 to 13 with a mean of 6.9. As for rank prior to becoming a police chief for the first time, 23 (39.7%) reported having been a deputy chief. The years of management experience before becoming a police chief ranged from 0 to 34 with a mean of 9.1 years. The ages of the respondents ranged from 37 to 67 years (mean = 49.9), 54 (93.1%) were white, 55 (93.8%) were male, and 24 (41.4%) possessed Masters' degrees (see Table 4.2).

Table 4-3 Selected Skills for Police Chief, Rank Order.*

Skill	Range	Mean	Mode	Median
Leadership	1–7	1.9	1.0	1.0
Communication	1–8	2.9	2.0	2.0
Decision-making	1–10	3.5	2.0	3.0
Organizational	1–9	4.2	3.0	3.0
Planning	1–9	4.6	5.0	5.0
Staffing	1–12	7.4	7.0	7.0
Budgeting	1–12	7.4	8.0	8.0
Discipline	3–12	8.1	9.0	10.0
Productivity	1–12	8.3	8.0	8.0
Labor relations	1–12	8.4	10.0	9.0
Job enrichment	1–12	9.2	11.0	10.0
Politics	0–12	9.5	12.0	11.0

* It should be noted that although all respondents rank-ordered these items, many did not complete a 1–12 ranking, but instead, ranked more than one at the same rank.

With respect to the police chief qualifications, twelve skills were offered for rank ordering from 1 to 12 (1 being most important). Leadership was found to be the most important skill with a mean of 1.9 (range 1 to 7, mode of 1.00). Politics was identified as the least required skill (mean = 9.5, range of 0 to 12, mode of 12.00) (see Table 4.3).

Of the employment criteria offered, police management experience was identified as the most important (mean of 2.00, range 1 to 9, mode of 1.00). The criterion considered the least important, at least by police chiefs in Cook County, Illinois, was graduation from the Southern Police Institute (mean of 8.1, range 1 to 10, mode of 10.00) (see Table 4.4).

Finally, respondents were asked to indicated whether hiring a police chief from inside or outside makes a difference. Although 22 (37.9%) thought that it did make a difference, their reason(s) why will be discussed in a future paper.

Table 4–4 Selected Required Criteria for Police Chief, Rank Order.*

Criterion	Range	Mean	Mode	Median
Police management experience	1–9	2.0	1.0	1.0
Extensive education and training	1–9	3.8	3.0	4.0
Record of continuous training	1–9	4.1	2.0	4.0
Knowledge of police science	1–10	4.8	4.0	4.0
Multi-ethnic community knowledge	1–10	4.9	3.0	5.0
Demonstrated experience with media	1–10	5.5	5.0	5.0
College degree	1–10	5.5	8.0	6.0
FBI graduation	1–10	7.0	9.0	8.0
College class in management	1–10	7.5	10.0	8.0
Southern Police Institute graduation	1–10	8.1	10.0	9.0

* It should be noted that although all respondents rank-ordered these items, many did not complete a 1–10 ranking, but instead, ranked more than one at the same rank.

DISCUSSION

There appears little doubt that the position of police chief requires scholarly study. The results reported here are only a beginning. Although these results may be useful in establishing current employment criteria for police chiefs, as well as what a sample of police chiefs indicate are most important—both as hiring requirements and skills they find important to possess as a police chief—they should be viewed as preliminary.

Police management experience was ranked the most important criterion for potential police chiefs. This was followed by extensive education and training. The police chiefs also ranked the skills a potential police chief should possess. The top five, beginning with most important, were leadership, communication, decison-making, organizational, and planning. A surprising result was the placement of political skill as the least important skill, particularly when it has been well-documented that most police chiefs must possess political savvy (Cox 1990). This tends to support findings by Witham (1986),

> Many law enforcement executives fail to realize that their positions entail political responsibilities as well as administrative duties. Although the "politics-administration" dichotomy has been rather thoroughly vanquished within public administration and police administration literature, the dichotomy is alive and well for many law enforcement leaders (p. 46).

It is obvious that the responding police chiefs somewhat agree with the advertisements as to important employment criteria for police chief. Police management experience appears to be the predominant requirement. Philosophically this makes sense. However, any astute observer of and participant in law enforcement would recognize the problems with this criterion, which are best represented by the following questions: What accounts for police managerial experience? Does simply climbing the promotional ladder qualify as police management experience? How and when are the skills required for police chief developed? With respect to police experience, how many years are really necessary? Isn't a general knowledge of policing satisfactory? Does it make a difference if the experience is with a small police agency or a large police agency?

Since college education requirements are increasing for the police recruit, it might be supposed that, police chiefs should be as, if not more highly, educated than the individuals they lead and manage. The police chiefs in this study indicated that the college degree wasn't highly necessary. Yet, the fact remains that among this sample of chiefs, a majority (48) of them possess a college degree, but lead agencies that do not require any college education for recruits or promotion. This finding in itself creates an interesting concern; however, this article will not pursue it.

Finally, what skills are the most important? Cox (1990) asks which is more important: policing skills or management skills? Although he does not answer it, Cox does note that answers to questions like this "are crucial in determining the criteria for promotion to leadership positions" (p. 175).

According to Witham (1987) there are four important developmental elements for successful police leadership: range of police and managerial experience, level of formal education, extent of professional development of training, and involvement with community and other groups outside law enforcement. Furthermore, Carter (1994) notes, from what he describes as "an exploratory and pedagogical exercise" (p. 9), involving a number of "middle managers and administrators of departments ranging in size from five officers to over 3,000 officers" (p. 9), the most frequently cited police management issue was the lack of vision by police leaders and leadership. While not explicitly stated in Carter's report, it may be reasonably assumed that his "leadership" refers to the types of elements noted by Witham.

The importance of the police chief to the police organization has been noted. Resources are available to assist in training and educating these significant police leaders. Yet, little has been done with respect to the examination of employment criteria for the position of police chief, or to verify their efficacy in the selection of effective police chiefs.

Many questions remained unanswered. The research at hand is one step toward inquiry into an arena that requires attention. An avenue of inquiry resulting from these findings is investigation of what appears to be the difference between what police chiefs themselves (at least in Cook County, Illinois) consider important employment criteria and the beliefs of theorists and reseachers. Obviously, additional research is required to explore why this difference exists. Furthermore, future research needs to identify and support employment criteria and requisite skills for police chiefs.

REFERENCES

Carter, D. L. (1994). Contemporary issues facing police administrators: Guideposts for the academic community. *Police Forum*, 4(1), 9–10.

——, and Sapp, A. D. (1990). The evolution of higher education in law enforcement: Preliminary findings from a national study. *Journal of Criminal Justice Education*, 1(1), 59–85.

Chandler, K. I. (1982). *A study of education of police chiefs in Illinois*. Unpublished Master's thesis, Western Illinois University, Macomb, IL.

Cox, S. M. (1990). Policing into the 21st century. *Police-Studies*, 13(4), 168–177.

Crank, J. P. (1987). *Professionalism among police chiefs*. Doctoral dissertation, University of Colorado.

Enter, J. E. (1986a). The role of higher education in the career of the American police chief. *Police-Studies*, 9(2), 110–119.

——. (1986b). The rise to the top: An analysis of police chief career patterns. *Journal of Police Science and Administration*, 14(4), 334–346.

Gaines, L. K., Southerland, M. D., and Angell, J. E. (1991). *Police Administration*. New York: McGraw-Hill.

Goldstein, H. (1977). *Policing a free society*. Cambridge, MA: Ballinger Publishing Co.

Hunt, R. G. and Magenau, J. M. (1993). *Power and the police chief*. Newbury Park, CA: Sage Publications.

Lynch, R. G. (1975). *The police manager*. Boston: Holbrook Press, Inc.

Maniha, J. K. (1973). Structural supports for the development of professionalism among police administrators. *Pacific Sociological Review*, 16(3), 315–343.

Masini, H. J. and Playfair, M. B. (1978). The nature of the police executive's role. *Police-Studies*, 1(2), 39–44.

Swanson, C. R., Territo, L., and Taylor, R. W. (1993). *Police Administration: Structures, processes, and behavior* (3rd ed). New York: Macmillan Publishing.

Wilson, O. W. and McLaren, R. C. (1977). *Police Administration* (4th ed). New York: McGraw-Hill.

Witham, D. C. (1985). *The American law enforcement chief executive: A management profile.* Washington, D.C.: Police Executive Research Forum.

———. (1986). Management reform and police executives. *The Bureaucrat,* 45–50.

———. (1987). Transformational police leadership. *FBI Law Enforcement Bulletin, 56*(12), 2–6.

Appendix

Police Chief Questionnaire

Please fill in or check off the appropriate responses. Thank you.

Agency Demographics

Department size : number sworn _____   number civilian _____

Population (Jurisdiction):   Department budget:

    under 10,000 _____   under 1 million _____

    10,001–25,000 _____   1–5 million _____

    25,001–50,000_____   6–10 million _____

    50,001–100,000 _____   over 10 million _____

    Over 100,000 _____

Education requirement for recruits:

    High school only _____

    Associate's degree _____

    Bachelor's degree _____

    No degree, but college hours: under 30 _____

                                30–60 _____

                                60–90 _____

                                other _____

Education requirements for promotion:

    None _____

    Associate's degree _____

    Bachelor's degree _____

    Other _____

Personal Demographics

How many years law enforcement experience? _____

How many years as a police chief of current department? _____

When hired as police chief, were you hired from within the department or from outside the department? _____

If hired from outside the department, had you been a police chief elsewhere? Yes _____ No _____

If yes, how many years had you been a police chief? _____

Prior to becoming a police chief for the first time, what was your highest rank attained?

Sergeant _____

Lieutenant _____

Captain _____

Deputy Chief _____

Other _____

Prior to becoming police chief for the first time, how many years police management experience did you have? _____

Your current age _____ Gender: Male _____ Female _____

Ethnicity: Caucasian _____ Asian _____

African American _____ Other _____

Hispanic _____

Highest level of education you have attained:

High school _____

Associate's degree _____

Bachelor's degree _____

Master's degree _____

Other _____

If you possess a college degree, what was your major? _____

Was your degree attained: pre-LEAA _____ LEAA _____ post-LEAA _____

Please list any other special qualifications you had prior to becoming a police chief (i.e., graduation from FBI National Academy) _____

_____
_____
_____
_____
_____
_____

Police Chief Qualifications

The following are skills identified as necessary for a police chief. Please rank from 1–12 by order of importance (1 being most important and 12 being the least important).

____ Organizational

____ Leadership

____ Planning

____ Communication

____ Decision-making

____ Budgeting

____ Productivity

____ Labor relations

____ Discipline

____ Job enrichment

____ Politics

____ Staffing

The following are items that have been found as requirements for potential police chiefs. Please rank in order of importance from 1–10 (1 being most important and 10 being least important).

_____ Record of continuous specialized training and educational achievement.

_____ Extensive education and training in police supervision.

_____ Demonstrated experience in media and community relations.

_____ Graduation from the FBI National Academy.

_____ Extensive knowledge of modern concepts and techniques in police science.

_____ Graduation from Southern Police Institute.

_____ Knowledge of or experience in law enforcement in a multi-ethnic community.

_____ Completion of 16 quarter hours or equivalent semester hours of college-level courses in supervisory management.

_____ College degree.

_____ Police management experience.

Based on your experience, what qualifications should a potential police chief possess? _____

_____

_____

_____

_____

_____

_____

_____

If a potential police chief candidate possesses the requested qualifications, does it make any difference if they are hired from within or from outside the agency?

Yes _____   No _____   Does not make a difference

_____

Why? _____
_____
_____
_____
_____
_____
_____
_____

AGAIN, THANK YOU FOR YOUR ASSISTANCE.

5

The Nature of Gang Violence*

Gerry Riposa and Carol Dersch

PREFACE

The most abhorrent aspect of urban gang subcultures is violence. Yet, too often the character of these antisocial, community damaging acts are overly sensationalized and understood at a surface level that often lacks more than anecdotal evidence. Operating from the premise that better policy responses are derived from better assessments of the problem, we decided to look at some of the more conventional generalizations about gang violence. Therefore, we chose a large city that has had an active gang subculture for the last fifteen years. After establishing the local context that contributes to the poverty that nutures youth gangs, we employed official statistics, coupled with face-to-face interviews, to portray a clearer picture of the realm and participants of urban gang violence.

---

* This article was previously published in the *Journal of Crime and Justice*, *XVIII*(2), 1995, pp. 31–46. It appears by permission of Anderson Publishing Company and the authors. All rights are reserved. No part of this article may be used or reproduced by any means without permission from the publisher.

We chose to use official statistics—knowing that there are some problems with reporting—because they offered a range of crimes over a period of time. From this data we could begin to draw a more accurate picture about the patterns and trends in gang violence. Other techniques were not useful, such as surveys, since gang members would be reluctant to disclose their participation, even if they could provide a full account of their behavior over the years of their membership. Interviewing gang members at the court house was also an option but required more time and resources than were available, and probably would not have provided the same spread of information we were looking for to begin generalizing about this subculture's violence. To enrich the data presentation we integrated field interviews where appropriate. Such interviews accentuate the clarity of a case study.

INTRODUCTION

While the literature suggests that violence plays an integral role in the gang subculture, few studies have dissected this aspect of gang life to expose its constitutive elements. The aim of this study is to first establish the socio-economic context which creates an environment conducive for the formation of violent street gangs; and second, to illustrate the violent activities in which they participate. By portraying a more accurate picture of gang violence (one that is neither romanticized nor sensationalized, but rather, grounded in actual activities), we provide a context that may assist policymakers in the development of more effective policies to counter this aspect of gang life (Gusfield 1989, 431).

Our central thesis is that gang violence demonstrates a character which is not a random series of anti-social acts. At odds with conventional notions, we suggest that this form of violence neither escalates in a unilinear way nor becomes pervasive across the gamut of gang criminal behavior. To explore this thesis, we examined the following questions: (1) In what forms is gang violence manifested? (2) Does gang violence demonstrate a general increase? and (3) Does gang violence permeate gang criminal behavior?

STUDY AND SETTING

The research reported here was conducted in Long Beach, California, between 1989 and 1993. The data were collected from the following sources:

- City of Long Beach Police Department.
- Direct interviews with current and former gang members, police officers assigned to gang neighborhoods, special officers in the city's Gang Suppression Unit, community and social service agencies, locally elected officials, teachers and administrators from the Long Beach School District, and the city's Gang Prevention Program.
- Secondary data from government documents, official statistics, and scholarly literature.

Data were also obtained from official crime statistics of the City of Long Beach Police Department, as well as from field interviews and from literature on gangs to heighten the explanatory power of the empirical data. We recognize and underscore that analysis of urban street gangs must not depend exclusively on officialdom's data banks, lest we fall into the trap of "courthouse sociology," as Hagedorn cautions (1990, 240).

The Setting

The City of Long Beach, incorporated in 1894, is the fifth largest city in California, second in size within L.A. county only to Los Angeles. From 1980 to 1990, the population has increased 19% to 422,433, which does not include a probable undercount of 22,000 residents (Long Beach Economic Forecasts 1993, 28). Mirroring the demographic trends of Los Angeles county and much of southern California, Long Beach reflects an increasingly multicultural population.

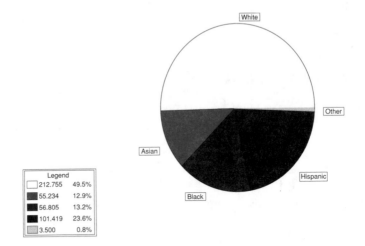

Figure 5.1 City of Long Beach Ethnic Diversity—1990 Census Data.

Because of race and class divisions, a sharp demarcation splits the city almost in half. Indeed, Long Beach can be characterized as two distinct cities. The eastside contains the majority of the Anglo population, exhibiting spatial patterns of low density and higher family median income (Long Beach Economic Forecasts 1993, 29). Vastly different, the westside is populated largely by working class and lower income blacks, Latinos, and southeast Asians (particularly Cambodians), living in denser housing conditions, with larger families, and on lower median incomes.

In concert with population increases in westside communities, sagging government revenues and growing unemployment have combined to reduce the capacity of city service delivery and outward migration through social mobility. During the period under study, although the national economy demonstrated moderate growth, California's economy, reeling from its worst recession since the 1930s, produced a 9.4% state unemployment rate and a 5% loss in the job base. Long Beach's economic condition was even worse. The city, whose primary industries are defense, government, and the service sector, experienced significant defense cutbacks, downsizing in the public and private sectors, and lukewarm retail consumption, resulting in a 10% unemployment rate and an 11% reduction in its job base (Long Beach Economic Forecast 1993).

Stagnant economic conditions have been felt across the city; yet, it is the westside which has absorbed the brunt of economic restructuring, resulting in higher and more prolonged unemployment, reduced city services, and increases in urban blight. For example, notwithstanding the city's loss of jobs, the average household income rose 28% between 1980 and 1990, but most of the benefits accrued to eastside neighborhoods. During this same period, the fraction of Long Beach's population slipping below the poverty line grew by 22%, a downward spiral almost exclusively affecting the residents of the westside.

This brief description portrays the economic and social context for our analysis on gang violence. Long Beach, caught in the grip of declining government revenues and economic transformation, manifests the familiar social model of growing disparities among its communities, exacerbated by race and class divisions. Gang violence percolates, festers, and erupts on the westside with regularity. Now such incidents are threatening other areas of the city with greater frequency.

PRINCIPLE FINDINGS

The Gangs

Since the 1950s, street gangs have existed, albeit on a small scale, in the urban culture of Long Beach. Having roots in car clubs, zoot suiters, and neighborhood corner gangs, these primarily working class and lower income youth associations remained small in size and operated at the periphery of the city. The 1980s, however, saw a complete break from this marginal presence in the urban milieu. The number of gangs multiplied, as did the membership. At the beginning of 1980, the city had approximately 13–16 street gangs with 800 members; by 1992 the numbers had increased to 70 gangs with roughly 12,700 members. This pattern of growth has occurred predominately in the African-American, Latino, and Cambodian communities, paralleling the overall growth in population and increasingly dense living conditions on the westside. One consequence of this growth in both population and street gangs has been escalated competition for scarce resources—territory, status, protection, and to some extent, drugs—in a contested urban space.

To provide some sense of this growth in the size and numbers of the city's street gangs, we have portrayed this increase in Table 5.1. All of the gangs noted here are classified under California's Street Terrorism Enforcement program [STEP] (see Appendix A for elaboration). Note that these estimated figures are derived from the county-wide Gang Reporting and Tracking System [GRAT] (see Appendix B for elaboration). Although we recognize that GRAT estimates are nothing moore than rough approximations, the tracking system does identify new gang "klikas and sets" and provides an indication of the escalating gang presence in the city.

The Violence

Since the 1960s, the arc of gang violence has risen. Our data appear to support this trend as gang violence is related to and accounts for a disproportionate share of the total gang incidents noted in Table 5.2. Specifically, homicides, drive-bys, and felony assaults—the engines of media attention and community fear—capture the largest share of this behavior, followed by shootings into buildings and misdemeanor assaults. Because these incidents demonstrate high levels of violence, it is not unexpected that moderate to serious injury has risen in concert with the rise of frequency and seriousness of violent gang acts. These data support conventional thinking about criminal gang behavior: that it is violent; it is escalating; and it is serious.

Without discounting the evidence indicating the degree of this problem in Long Beach, a closer look suggests other significant qualifications that are not normally part of the discourse on street gang violence. For example, gang violence does not involve a wide

Table 5-1 Long Beach Gangs Covered in the Street Terrorism Enforcement Gang Program (STEP).*

Name of Gang	Number of Members	
	1991	1992
East Side Longos	1,402	1,645
Insane Crips	1,277	1,389
West Side Longos	753	822
East Side Paramount	414	424
Rollin' 20's Crips	391	438
Sons of Samoa	390	422
Barrio Small Town	307	359
Barrio Pobre	239	333
Tiny Rascal Gang	155	246
Asian Boyz	102	157
Tray Loc Crips	20	20
Totals	5,450	6,255

* Statistics provided by the Gang Investigations Unit, Long Beach Police Department. [Note: During the same period of time, the Los Angeles County Sheriff's Department Gang Reporting and Tracking System (GRAT) was tracking the criminal activities of 11,000 gang members (1991) and 12,719 gang members (1992)].

range of criminal acts. A lack of gang involvement in other potentially violent acts—arson, kidnapping, witness intimidation, rape/attempted rape, other felony sex crimes, and assault on a police officer—contradicts the public's perception of increasing gang violence. More importantly, if one looks across all the criminal categories, including those patently violent acts noted earlier, we see that the numbers of incidents have either remained firm or have experienced some decline in the last two years of this study. This observation calls into question the perception that gang violence is both a pervasive and an escalating monolithic phenomenon.

Table 5-2 Gang-Related Crime in Long Beach, 1989–1992.

Type of Crime	1989	1990	1991	1992
Total Crime and Narcotics	1,013	1,172	844	664
Homicide	16	36	40	46
Felony Assault	192	266	200	166
Misdemeanor Assault	66	54	42	24
Rape/Attempted Rape	6	15	8	0
Shooting into Buildings	69	113	57	30
Robbery	78	101	82	79
Kidnapping	5	0	3	1
Assault on Officer	2	1	2	5
Arson	0	0	1	3
Witness Intimidation	2	0	4	7
Extortion	1	4	1	2
Arrest-St. Terrorism Act	0	78	164	5
Weapon Law Violation	28	24	24	18
Burglary	24	49	22	21
Grand Theft Auto	35	27	1+	19
Receiving Stolen Property	6	6	2+	0
Other Felony Sex Crime	3	6	1+	0
Vandalism	238	130	3+	76
Drunkenness	8	10	0+	0
All Other Crime	137	127	16+	37
Moderate-Serious Injury	153	151	10+	192
Drive-by	NA*	NA*	121	107

Source: Long Beach Police Department (Statistics reported to Los Angeles County Sheriff's Department).

* statistics not kept for this crime during 1989 and 1990.

+ statistics in these types of crimes compiled only for January 1991.

Moreover, categorizing by specific acts of violence indicates the elements that constitute this behavior in the gang subculture.

Tools of Violence

No analysis of gang violence can ignore the perception of the marauding gangster wielding an automatic assault weapon. To be sure, our field and empirical analyses demonstrate that usage and sophistication of weaponry proliferated and escalated (Interviews

Table 5–3 Weapons Used in Gang-Related Violence 1989–1992.

Weapons	1989	1990	1991	1992
Handguns	82	172	211	182
Shotguns	18	14	15	8
Rifles	7	7	3	1
Assault Weapons	4	3	3	0
Unknown	57	95	48	54
Cutting/Stabbing	17	21	18	40
Other Weapons	44	40	72	85
Total Firearms	168	291	280	245
Total Weapons	229	352	369	345

Statistics reported by Long Beach Police Department to Los Angeles County Sheriff's Department on a monthly basis January 1989–December 1992.

with gang members 1989–1992). As one gang member seemed to sum up the sentiment of a number of our respondents, "man, it's just like a (expletive) arms race, if you don't carry, you get smoked. You know man, like you will be looking to get listed as a 187." Nevertheless, rather than AK-47s, Uzis, and AR-15s, handguns, more than all other weapons combined, command center stage in this deadly aspect of the gang culture.

Although, these findings do not negate the occasional use of automatic weapons in the city's gang environment, nor discount the storage of such weapons until exceptionally perceived circumstances demand use. They do, however, focus our attention on the primary weapon of violence. Field interviews shed additional light on the choice of handguns by gang members. Noting the expense and lack of accuracy of automatic weapons, respondents related that accessibility and control when firing on the move made handguns appealing. Even more important, respondents confided that handguns are easy to carry, allowing a better chance to get close to an enemy, fire and then escape. Besides utility, handguns (particularly 9 mm.), not rifles or assault weapons, are status symbols; "the tools," to be displayed and admired as badges of power (Interviews with gang members 1989–1992).

Also neglected in most descriptions of current gang violence is the continued use of non-powered hand weapons: pipes, knives, car antennas, nunchucks (karate sticks), and baseball bats. These weapons, as a category, figure second compared to hand guns. Although less glamorous, these weapons are most accessible and usually are the instruments of spontaneous violence, such as gang-on-gang conflict to defend territory and remedy acts of disrespect (Interviews with gang members 1989–1992).

Weapons are the instruments of violence and also are, in the case of handguns, symbols of status. To properly frame the problem of gang violence, it is necessary to understand that handguns are the principal agents of injury and means for exacerbating the scope and degree of violence.

Soldiers of Violence

Because the age range of gang membership has expanded to include a cohort ranging from 12 to 27 years, the widely held assumption suggests that adult presence and influence on younger members propels gang violence: either adults are more likely to commit violence or adults are more likely to persuade younger members to commit crimes and act as "triggers," or younger members are more likely to try to impress the OGs (original gangsters or older gangsters) or *veteranos*.

To examine the possibility of a membership age pattern in this violence, we have drawn on criminal arrest reports, coupled with field interviews, based on the following reasoning. Because a disproportionate number of crimes are violent, and a disproportionate number of arrests—while not displayed in the tables—fall within these violent crimes, we argue that these arrests act as an unobtrusive measure of who is primarily involved in gang violence in Long Beach.

For the first two years of the study, with the exception in vandalism, adults exceeded juveniles in criminal incident arrests. This pattern shifted dramatically in 1991 as juveniles incurred the

Table 5–4 Juvenile/Adult Gang Arrest Statistics 1989–1992.

Type of Incidents	1989	1990	1991	1992
Crime Incidents	947	1,121	784	650
Adult Arrests	167	191	116	127
Juvenile Arrests	153	113	193	143
Narcotic Incidents	60	51	77	14
Adult Arrests	34	36	22	22
Juvenile Arrests	32	17	37	10
Total Gang Incidents	1,013	1,172	844	664
Adult Arrests	201	237	148	147
Juvenile Arrests	185	160	230	153

Statistics reported by Long Beach Police Department to Los Angeles Police Department, 1989–1992.

majority of arrests, most of which were included within the violent crime categories displayed in Table 5.2. Understandably, one could argue that adult gang members were participating in violent crimes but due to experience were more elusive and less prone to brag about their exploits. This is plausible; yet our field interviews support the findings in Table 5.4. First, gang membership encourages both adults and youths to discuss their acts of violence in order to develop status within the gang and community. Just as important, while extended adult membership from marginalization and unemployment is a continuing dynamic in the gang subculture, as noted by Horowitz (1982), Long Beach street gangs are predominantly youth gangs.

Because they comprise the majority of membership, juveniles predominate in violent acts. Both adult and youth respondents of the study admitted that at times older members planned actions and influenced youth participation; yet, this situation occurred intermittently. The split in the data in Table 5.4 is perhaps better explained by changes in the city's gang culture. As gangs have expanded, primarily through youth recruitment, larger numbers of younger members have sought to establish their own reputations as being "down" with the set or barrio, and, as part of that process, to gain respect from the older members and their own peers.

Drugs and Violence

No issue is perceived as more intertwined in the street gang culture than drugs and drug trafficking. Media, entertainment, and our interviews with elected officials and members of public agencies in Long Beach and L.A. county demonstrated unanimous agreement on this point (Interviews with City Council and City Manager 1989, 1992; Thomas White, Director, Gang Prevention Services 1990–1993; and Norm Sorenson, head of LBPD Gang Suppression Unit 1989–1992). For example, the head of the Long Beach Gang Suppression Unit, a twenty-year veteran of the police department and gang work, stated that "ninety-five percent of all gang members are involved in drug and alcohol abuse, or the sale, transportation, and manufacture of drugs." These sorts of declarations, common in our interviews with city officials and police, were rarely supported by empirical evidence.

Our field research found that gang members use drugs and alcohol liberally; some to the point of abuse. But do drugs and drug trafficking relate to gang violence in the city? Here the use of official statistics allows us to draw some inference. When drug possession or sales is the primary criminal offense, the perpetrator is processed by the Narcotics Bureau, which neither identifies nor records that person by gang relatedness or affiliation. On the other hand, if a gang member is arrested for a primary offense, such as those noted in Table 5.2, and he or she also is involved in a drug-related offense, the offense is then recorded as a gang statistic under narcotic incidents, which are reported in our study. This separation accounts for the relatively few narcotic offenses in the data in Table 5.4.

Although the connection between drugs and gang violence cannot be clearly illustrated by our data, some general impressions do emerge. Across our gang interviews, black, Latino, and Asian respondents acknowledged some drug use and dealing in their respective gangs. This behavior was especially evident among members of Crip sets, but was increasingly prevalent among Latino and southeast Asian gangs. Nevertheless, only black gang members stated that they felt that drugs and the competition for dominance in distribution generated violence; and even then, they noted that general disputes over control of territory (including key locations such as shopping malls or gyms) as well as acts of disrespect and retaliation also contributed to violence. Latino and southeast Asian gang members discounted drugs as the main agents causing violence; instead, they cited control of territory such as local high schools and parks, and acts of robbery and retaliation. Table 5.4 provides indirect evidence supporting other causes of gang violence by indicating a far smaller number of drug-involved gang offenses. Thus, the accepted linkage between drugs and gang violence is at least questionable.

CONCLUSION

Perspectives on street gang violence are both accurate and confused. Amidst views containing elements of accuracy lie stereotypes which can cloud our understanding of this dimension in gang culture, eventually leading decision-makers to enact misguided policies. A more approximate picture, however, is possible. This case study supports the conventional perspective that gang violence exists at intolerable levels. The Long Beach experience, at first glance, fits the commonly held image of homicides, drive-bys, assaults, and robberies as the dominant expressions of street gang violence.

However, this view does not provide the entire picture. A more qualified assessment is demanded. When violence does occur in the city's gang culture, it is traceable to juvenile members, acting in an environment where adult influences and expectations are present, coupled with a youthful desire to establish one's own reputation and acquire social status. This contradicts the public's view of adult-orchestrated violence carried out by overly compliant and malleable youths. Not automatic rifles, but handguns serve as the principle tool of violence, out-distancing all other weapons. Although the study does not discount the commonly perceived linkage between drugs and gang violence, it at least questions this relationship as the foundation of gang violence.

More important in this examination of the nature of gang violence is identification of the arenas in which violence does not occur. Not dismissing the impact of violence on the community and gang members themselves, these acts, which do make up the majority of total crime incidents, occur in a relatively small number of categories. Thus the idea is suspect that gang violence and general illegal behavior are rampant across a wide range of behaviors. Even more significant, however, this case study casts doubt on the perception of a continuous escalation of violence; rather, the evidence suggests that most street gang criminal behavior, including that which encompasses the most violent acts, has either remained static, or shown some decline.

REFERENCES

Chin, K. (1990). "Chinese Gangs and Extortion." In *Gangs in America*, C.R. Huff (ed.). Newbury Park, CA: Sage.

Fagen, J. (1989). "The Social Organization of Drug Use and Drug Dealing Among Urban Gangs." *Criminology* 27:633–669.

Gusfield, J. R. (1989). "Constructing the Ownership of Social Problems: Fun and Profit in the Welfare State." *Social Problems* 36:431–441.

Hagedorn, J. M. (1988). *People and Folks: Gangs, Crime and the Underclass in a Rustbelt City*. Milwaukee: University of Wisconsin Press, Milwaukee.

Hagedorn, J. M. (1990). "Back in the Field Again: Gang Research in the Nineties." In *Gangs in America*, C. R. Huff (ed.). Newbury Press, CA: Sage.

Horowitz, R. (1982). "Adult Delinquent Gangs in the Chicano Community: Masked Intimacy and Marginality." *Urban Life* 11:3–26.

Horowitz, R. (1990). "Sociological Perspective on Gangs: Conflicting Definitions and Concepts." In *Gangs in America,* edited by C. R. Huff. Newbury Press, CA: Sage.

Huff, C. R. (1989). "Youth Gangs and Public Policy." *Journal of Crime and Delinquency* 35:524–537.

Huff, C. R. (1990). "Two Generations of Gang Research." In *Gangs in America*, C. R. Huff (ed.). Newbury Park, CA: Sage.

Katz, J. (1990). *Seductions of Crime.* New York: Basic Books.

Klein, M. W. and Maxon, C. L. (1985). "'Rock Sales' in South Los Angeles." *Sociology and Social Research* 69:561–565.

Miller, W. B. (1990). "Why the United States Has Failed to Solve its Youth Gang Problem." In *Gangs in America*, C. R. Huff (ed.). Newbury Press, CA: Sage.

More, J. W. (1978). *Homeboys: Gangs, Drugs, and Prisons in the Barrios of Los Angeles.* Philadelphia: Temple University Press.

Office of Economic Research (1993). *Long Beach Economic Forecasts,* 1993 (Third Annual Report). Long Beach, CA: Department of Economics California State University, Long Beach.

Padilla, F. M. (1992). *The Gang as an American Enterprise.* New Brunswick, NJ: Rutgers University Press.

Riposa, G. and C. Dersch (1990). "Urban Street Gangs as Political Actors: No Longer the Off, Off Broadway Show." Paper presented at the Annual Political Science Association meeting, San Franciseo, CA.

Rodriguez, L. J. (1993). "Young People Without Options—They Keep Killing Themselves." *Los Angeles Times,* March 7, 1993: 3M.

Sanchez-Jankowski, M. (1991). *Islands in the Street: Gangs in American Urban Society.* Berkeley: University of California.

Santoli, A. (1991). "What Can be Done About Gangs?" *Parade,* March 24, 1991: 16–19.

Spergel, I. A. (1984). "Violent Gangs in Chicago: In Search of Social Policy." *Social Service Review* 58: 199–226.

Spergel, I. A. (1985). *The Violent Gang Problem in Chicago.* Chicago: University of Chicago, School of Social Service Administration.

Taylor, C. S. (1990). *Dangerous Society.* East Lansing: Michigan State University.

Torres, V. (1992). "2 Hurt in Gang Gunfire at Mall in West Covina." *Los Angeles Times,* February 26, 1992: 1A, 12A.

Vigil, J. D. (1988). *Barrio Gangs: Street Life and Identity in Southern California.* Austin: University of Texas Press.

Appendix A

Street Terrorism Enforcement Program

California's Street Terrorism Enforcement Program, established by the Street Terrorism Enforcement and Prevention Act of 1988, identifies particular gangs with reputations for violence and crime as 'criminal gang' and makes membership a felony. The law prosecutes any person who actively participates in such a gang with the knowledge that its members have engaged in a pattern of criminal gang activity, and who willfully promotes or assists any felonious conduct by members of that gang. In addition, this program provides for enhanced sentences for members of these designated gangs if arrested and convicted.

Appendix B

Gang Reporting and Tracking System

Los Angeles County's Gang Reporting and Tracking System (GRAT) is the central computer data base used to monitor gang size and presence in both the larger and individual communities. Individuals are entered into this system if arrested and self-identify or if identified by others as a gang member. Also, if an officer questions a person on the street who admits membership in a particular gang, a card is filled out on the person and the information is later entered into the data bank. Problems with the system are numerous. For example, the chances of duplication of field cards exists as gang members can be interviewed at various times, giving different information in each instance. Or, if a group of individuals are questioned on the street, and one is identified as a gang member, cards are filled out on all the individuals and entered into the gang data base. Also, names are not deleted from the data bank for five years, regardless of relocation outside the area or cessation of gang involvement. Although flawed, the system does provide an estimate of gang presence in a community, though not necessarily evidence of residency. Because most gangs have some territorial base, once identified they can be connected to a particular community.

6

The Legacy of Domestic Violence:
Juvenile Delinquency*

Philip W. Rhoades and Sharon L. Parker

PREFACE

The underlying purpose of this research was to determine the extent of experience with domestic violence on the part of delinquent juveniles incarcerated in the State of Oregon. The information was sought to support an effort to improve the networking between domestic violence and youth serving agencies within the state. Networking is believed necessary because of the growing evidence that these two social problems, domestic violence and juvenile delinquency, are related. Indeed, a direct causal link between domestic violence and later juvenile delinquency has been suggested. Helfer and Kempe (1976) observed that "the effects of child abuse and neglect are cumulative," which damages child

* Funding was provided by the Department of Health and Human Services (Grant 10-4-1-80101). An earlier version of this paper was presented at the meeting of the Academy of Criminal Justice Sciences at Louisville, KY in March 1982.

development and, thus, a large majority of delinquent adolescents indicate that they were abused children.

This article provides some speculative theoretical groundwork for this link using the social control, differential association, and labeling theories. Development and testing of this theoretical link is necessary to support improvements in society's understanding and response to both domestic violence and juvenile delinquency; chi square allowed us to examine those possible causal links.

INTRODUCTION

Evidence linking domestic violence and delinquency comes from a comparison of the hospital records of delinquent and nondelinquent children (Lewis and Shanock 1979), tracing official records of abused children and delinquents (Alfaro 1978), and interviews of juveniles detained by police (Steele 1976, 20). Each of these studies demonstrated a statistical link between juvenile delinquency and child abuse. Smith, Berkman, and Fraser (1980) reviewed these and other studies and found that this statistical link is well established.

The present study contributes to the weight of these findings. A survey questionnaire was administered at one nonresidential and five residential juvenile treatment programs during the spring and summer of 1981. The residential facilities included a large, cottage-based facility for males, a coed dormitory-high school facility, the Juvenile Treatment Unit at the State Hospital, and two small halfway houses. All of the juveniles had been originally placed in the programs by order of a court. Several had remained in treatment voluntarily, beyond the jurisdiction of the court. Each of the programs was visited by the research team at the time convenient to the agency. Considerable negotiation was required to obtain limited access to administer the questionnaire. The juveniles were given a brief oral and written description of the project and could decline to participate by so marking an informed consent document. While the programs contained 613 juveniles, access was limited by the agencies to 275 and only 191 volunteered to complete the questionnaire.

Therefore, the sample is 69.4% of those juveniles to whom access was provided and 31.2% of those in the programs at the time of the study.

The juveniles were asked questions about their involvement in sixteen types of delinquency, family characteristics, the behavior of their male and female primary parents towards them while the parent was angry, and their observation of spousal abuse. Thus, a voluntary, nonrandom sample of 191 juveniles was obtained of which 58.1% (111) were male and 40.3% (77) were female (3 failed to respond). The respondents ages ranged from twelve to twenty-three with a mean age of sixteen. The respondents were predominantly white, 79.6%, with 10.5% Native American, 3.7% Black, and 2.6 % Hispanic (3.7% unknown). The respondents reported living with between 1 and 57 parent figures with a mean of 7.6. Respondents listing only one parent figure totalled 6%, two parent figures 18%, and 3 or 4 parent figures 20%. The 37.2% of the sample who had lived in numerous foster home placements account for the large range and the high average number of parent figures.

The juveniles reported participation in from one to sixteen different types of delinquency (see Table 6.1) ranging from runaway to murder with an average of eight. The types of delinquency reported varied due to sex.

Males demonstrated more involvement in violent offenses and females more involvement in victimless offenses. Some of these differences were significant when tested by chi square, as indicated on Table 6.1. However, no difference in the average number of delinquent acts was found due to sex, age, or ethnicity.

The juveniles reported considerable experience with domestic violence, as noted on Tables 6.2 and 6.3. A surprising 68.0% reported abusive discipline (kicking, hitting with a fist, and hitting or threatening with an object) from either one or both parents. When slapping and pushing were added, 85.8% reported experiencing physical discipline. Male parents were reported to use the most serious physical and abusive discipline more frequently than female parents. In addition to the data on these tables, 36.6% reported witnessing spouse abuse by their male parent and 18.8%

Table 6–1 Reported Participation in Delinquency (N = 191).

Type of Crime	Number	% of Sample	% of Male	% of Female
Runaway	150	78.5	68.5	92.2*
Suicide	69	36.1	18.9	59.7*
Prostitution	27	14.1	2.7	29.9*
Drug Use	170	89.0	87.4	90.0
Alcohol Use	173	90.6	91.0	90.9
Shoplifting	175	91.6	91.0	92.2
Credit Card Theft	58	30.4	34.2	24.7
Auto Theft	112	58.6	67.6	45.5*
Other Theft	138	72.3	75.7	67.5
Forgery	78	40.8	41.4	40.3
Breaking and Entering	142	74.3	83.8	61.0*
Vandalism	130	68.1	77.5	55.8*
Arson	57	29.8	33.3	24.7
Assault	120	62.8	61.3	66.2
Rape	14	7.3	12.6	0
Murder	13	6.8	9.9	2.6
Other	29	15.2	16.2	14.3

* Value of chi square significant at p = .005 level.

by their female parent. It is clear that a large number of these juvenile delinquents had experienced and observed domestic violence.

However, despite this type of statistical linkage, little effort has been made to integrate the knowledge into the more traditional theories of the causes of juvenile delinquency. Such integration appears possible due to the emphasis on learning processes found both in the domestic violence and juvenile delinquency literature.

LEARNING DOMESTIC VIOLENCE

The family is the social unit where norms and behaviors are taught. It is the primary place where socialization occurs

Table 6-2 Frequency of Father's Behavior Toward Respondents When Angry By Percentage Reporting (N = 191).*

| | | | Times Behavior Occurred Per Year | | | |
| | | | Less | | | More |
Behavior	Never	Missing	than 1	1-6	6-12	than 12
Talked calmly	26.7	16.2	10.5	15.2	7.9	23.6
Took privilege	19.9	12.1	7.3	17.3	8.4	35.1
Yelled	8.9	13.1	2.6	11.0	9.4	55.0
Called names	32.5	13.1	5.2	9.4	4.7	35.1
Pushed	29.3	12.6	11.0	12.0	6.3	28.8
Slapped	24.6	11.0	10.5	18.3	4.7	30.9
Kicked	56.0	14.7	4.2	7.9	3.7	13.6
Punched with fist	50.8	14.7	7.3	9.9	3.1	14.1
Scared with object	53.9	16.3	5.2	6.8	4.2	13.6
Hit with object	43.5	14.6	3.7	9.4	7.3	15.7

* Percentages total across rows to 100.

(Campbell 1974, 252), which helps determine the individual's future behavior patterns (Sutherland and Cressey 1970, 203). The literature on domestic violence offers the theory that domestic violence is passed from generation to generation through the learning by imitation, modeling, and identification that occurs in families (Steele 1976, 21-22; Fontana, 1976; Steinmetz and Straus 1974, 20-21).

Domestic violence in the form of physical punishment and abuse of children appears to increase their aggressive tendencies, which may, in turn, lead to additional punishment or abuse (Sears, Maccoby, and Levin 1974; Steinmetz and Straus 1974, 3). Steele (1976, 14-15) notes that the most consistent finding about parents who maltreat their children has been that they were maltreated as children. Steinmetz (1977a; 1977b) notes that children tend to adopt the same form of conflict resolution that their parents used. These conclusions receive support from research that traced the family histories of abused children (Oliver and Taylor 1971),

Table 6-3 Frequency of Mothers' Behavior Toward Respondents When Angry By Percentage Reporting (N = 191).*

Behavior	Never	Missing	Less than 1	1-6	6-12	More than 12
					Times Behavior Occurred Per Year	
Talked calmly	18.8	9.4	3.1	15.7	8.4	44.5
Took privilege	24.1	7.3	7.9	21.5	11.5	27.7
Yelled	18.8	5.7	7.3	14.7	14.7	38.7
Called names	44.5	10.4	8.4	9.9	3.1	23.6
Pushed	54.5	7.8	7.9	8.9	5.8	15.2
Slapped	37.2	7.8	13.1	16.2	8.4	17.3
Kicked	75.4	9.4	2.1	4.2	106	7.3
Punched with fist	71.2	9.4	4.7	3.1	4.2	7.3
Scared with object	64.4	11.5	5.2	6.3	3.1	9.4
Hit with object	59.2	12.5	5.2	7.9	3.1	12.0

* Percentages total across rows to 100.

examined the type of discipline experienced by abusing parents (Smith and Hanson 1975), inquired about the behavior of the parents of fathers who have murdered their children (Scott 1973), and surveyed the violent behavior of incarcerated delinquents (Kratcowski and Kratcowski 1983).

Additionally, violence learned in the home is transferred to the interpersonal relationships that children have outside the home. The presence of domestic violence in the histories of children who have attempted or committed murder has been repeatedly documented (Bender and Curran 1946; Easson and Steinhilber 1961; Sargent 1962; Sendi and Blomgren 1975; Sorrells 1977; Tanay 1973; Corder et al. 1976). Similar findings occur in the examination of the childhood of adult murderers. They appear to have learned to live violently as children (Duncan et al. 1958; Bach-y-Rita and Veno 1974). The conclusion has been reached that violence is a behavior that is learned in the family as a "means of problem solving" (Steele 1976, 23; Steinmetz and Straus 1974, 231–236).

Violent behavior is only part of the legacy that domestic violence leaves for society. Domestic violence may be a major factor in the causation of many forms of juvenile delinquency and adult criminality. This can be demonstrated by discussing the phenomenon of domestic violence in relation to the social control and differential association theories of delinquency for these involve learning in the family as a causal mechanism.

DOMESTIC VIOLENCE AS EVIDENCE OF SOCIAL CONTROL THEORY

The theory of juvenile delinquency best supported by the data is social control. Control theories contend that social behavior results from the training or socialization of the individual. Delinquency results from defective socialization, largely defective rearing in the family (Nettler 1974, 216–17, 236). Hirschi (1971, 16–26) states that delinquent acts may occur when the individual's bond to society and its norms is weak or broken. The major element in bonding is the attachment one has to the norms and behaviors acceptable to society through one's affective ties (Hirschi 1971, 18). Weakening of this attachment through disruptions in the socialization process within the home may contribute to delinquency.

Broken homes have been one of the major indicators used to examine the individual's attachment. Yet, reviews of the literature about the effect of broken homes on delinquency have found little support for the causal link (Sutherland and Cressey 1970, 207–208; Peterson and Becker 1965, 68–70; Grinnell and Chambers 1979; Hennessy, Richards, and Berk 1978, 520).

This result may occur because the broken home indicator is not an adequate measure of attachment. Broken homes may not necessarily be unhappy homes. Of more importance is internal discord and tension, which may exist in either broken or intact homes (Hennessy, Richards, and Berk 1978, 506; Nye 1958;

Peterson and Becker 1965, 69–70), and "the quality of training and the content of the lessons taught that are the important determinants of lawful behavior" (Nettler 1974, 244).

Three factors were chosen to indicate family stability: the type of parent figures noted as primary parents, the number of parent figures lived with, and the size of the family. The respondents noted an average of 7.6 parent figures (individuals acting in a parental role). Of the sample, 48.2% reported living with a stepfather, 22.0% with a stepmother, 37.3% with a male guardian, 45.5% with a female guardian, and 37.2% with a foster parent.

No difference was found in the average number of types of delinquency reported between those who had lived with only natural parents and those who had lived with other types of parent figures. No relationship was found between family size and the average number of delinquency types reported. However, the number of parent figures was associated in a positive direction (Pearson's $r = .2180$, $p = .002$) to delinquency. This association may stem from the large number of foster home placements experienced by seventy of the juveniles, and it cannot be determined if placements occurred before or after the delinquency began. Therefore, it was concluded that the indicators of family stability were not strongly related to delinquency.

Marital instability appears to be related to domestic violence because it generally occurs prior to the violence (Pemberton and Benaday 1973; O'Neill et al. 1973). Although domestic violence may contribute to the dissolution of homes, some violent homes remain intact. Spouses may remain for extended periods in abusive situations (Langley and Levy 1978). Spousal abuse may actually be a stabilizing factor through a reduction of the tension and provision of a temporary solution to problems. Similarly, child abuse acts to delay a final resolution to environmental, emotional, and economic stresses that contribute to violence (Justice and Justice 1976).

To test for an association between family stability and domestic violence, a summary scale for the physical discipline methods and interactions between spouses (a scale of spousal abuse) was created based on the frequency of occurrence per year. Data were collected for each of four physical interactions based on five categories of frequency per year (i.e., never, less than once a year, 1 to 6, 7 to 12, more than 12). The frequency category (0 to 4) was used as a simple additive scale of physical interactions (0 to 16) for each of four possible pairs: male and female parent to child, male to female parent, and female to male parent. When added together, these scales resulted in individual parent behavior scales (0 to 32) and a summary scale (0 to 64) of the experience and observation of violence for each respondent. A positive association (Pearson's $r = .3977$ for male parent, $.1911$ for female parent, and $.3619$ for the combined scale; all at $p = .005$) between these scales of domestic violence and the number of parent figures was found. Thus, the greater the family instability, the greater the domestic violence.

Natural fathers were reported to be abusive by 55.1% and natural mothers by 35.9%, while other male parent figures were reported to be abusive by 71.4% and other female parent figures by 47.4%. A test for the difference between proportions was used. The difference for the male parents was found to be significant ($p = .025$), but that for the female parents was not.

Family stability, as measured by these variables, shows some positive association to domestic violence. One conclusion from this data is that domestic violence may be a better indicator of the attachment element of control theory than broken homes because it may be a better measure of the tension and discord that weaken elements of bond (i.e., attachment). Further, domestic violence is a measure of behavior that may be found in both intact and broken homes.

Control theorists argue that norms and behavior patterns are learned through operant conditioning in the form of parental discipline and through modeling of the parents' behavior (Nettler 1974, 216–26). However, punitive forms of discipline have been related to hostile, aggressive, violent, and delinquent behavior on the part of the recipients (McCord and McCord 1958; Peterson and Becker 1964, 82–87; Bandura and Walters 1958, 64). Physical discipline may interfere with the development of the attachment or belief elements of bond. Bandura and Walters (1958, 52, 65) note that physical discipline may disrupt the dependency relationship and reduce the identification with the parents that is necessary for learning of norms. Campbell (1974, 258) argues that the parents may teach one set of rules (nonviolence) and behave by another (violence), and thus, cause conflict in the perceptions of the child that hinders the norm-sending process.

Learning of behavior seems to occur through observation and imitation. To learn from a model, one may need to perceive the model as "competent or prestigious" (Nettler 1974, 222, 226) or merely successful in solving the immediate problem. Physical discipline of children may fail to teach morality because of its punitive and rejecting qualities (Nettler 1974, 225–26). However, it does teach the use of violence because it is a successful behavior. Hirschi (1971, 202) comments that the state of anomie has been reached when only questions of expediency are considered prior to violation of a law. Juveniles from violent homes may fail to form attachment to, and belief in, the prosocial norms of their parents. Instead, they may only acquire the behaviors that are expedient in solving problems. If this is occurring, the most delinquent juveniles should also be the most physically disciplined and abused. To begin to test this, the number of types of delinquency variables was dicotomized into high and low groups at the mean. These groups were then compared by the type of discipline experienced. The results are found on Table 6.4. Juveniles reporting a higher degree of delinquency reported a higher degree of abusive behavior from both parent figures. The results for the male parent demonstrated an association with a low statistical significance.

The parent's method of discipline was dicotomized into nonphysical and physical categories to reduce the effects of small cells in tabular analysis. This revealed that 69.8% of the nonphysical discipline group reported a high level of delinquency, but 80.9% of the physical discipline group reported a high level in relation to the

Table 6–4 Extent of Delinquency by Method of Parent's Discipline.

| Method of Discipline | Number of Delinquent Acts | | | |
	Low		High	
Male Parent*	N	%	N	%
Never	11	12.8	10	9.5
Non-Physical	15	17.4	10	9.5
Physical	19	22.1	16	15.2
Abusive	41	47.7	69	65.7
Totals:	86	100.0	105	100.0
Female Parent				
Never	11	12.8	4	3.8
Non-Physical	22	25.6	26	24.8
Physical	23	26.7	30	28.6
Abusive	30	34.8	45	42.9
Totals:	86	100.0	105	100.0

* chi square = 6.6 with P = .09; Cramer's V = .1859.

male parent's discipline. The figures were 61.6% and 71.4% respectively for the female parent discipline groups. The difference for the male parent group's was significant at the .08 level with chi square at 3.23 and a contingency coefficient of .1823. That for the female parent was not significant (chi square = 2.05, contingency coefficient = .1459). The data weakly indicate that the more physically disciplined were also the more delinquent.

To examine observation of domestic violence, the parents' behavior toward each other was compared to the juvenile's participation in delinquency (see Table 6.5). While only a minority of juveniles observed either form of spouse abuse, a greater proportion of those who were in the high delinquency group had observed domestic violence than those in the low delinquency group. This finding is significant for the male parent data.

Further evidence of the positive association between both the experience and observation of domestic violence and delinquency

Table 6-5 Extent of Participation in Delinquency by Observation of Spousal Abuse.

Behavior Toward Spouse	Reported Delinquency			
	Low		High	
Male Parent*	N	%	N	%
Not Abusive	65	75.6	56	53.3
Abusive	21	24.4	49	46.7
Totals:	86	100.0	105	100.0
Female Parent**				
Not Abusive	75	87.2	80	76.2
Abusive	11	12.8	25	23.8
Totals:	86	100.0	105	100.0

* chi square = 9.14 with P = .0025; contingency coefficient .2239.
** chi square = 3.06 with P = .08; contingency coefficient .1388.

was obtained through the use of the scales previously discussed. It was found that the male parent's behavior was positively related to the number of reported delinquent acts with a Pearson's r of .229 and the female parent's behavior at .207 (p = .002).

The scales for the parent's behavior were each modified into indicators of both seriousness and frequency. It was assumed that the seriousness of the physical interaction would have an additive effect. Therefore, the categories of interaction were condensed into four (0 = none, 1 = slap or punch, 2 = kick, and 3 = strike with an object). This measure was multiplied by the frequency measure, which resulted in very simplistic scales (0 to 96) of both seriousness and frequency of the experienced and observed violence. These new scales were also significantly related in a positive direction to the number of delinquent acts reported (Pearson's r = .198 for the female parent and .218 for the male parent; p = .003). The domestic violence scales indicate that the more frequent and more serious the domestic violence, the greater the number of types of delinquency committed by the respondents.

Although the statistical associations reported above are small, the direction of the relationships is consistently positive. Juveniles who had experienced and observed more frequent and more serious domestic violence reported a greater involvement in delinquency.

The data seem to support the theory that it is the failure to form attachment to and belief in prosocial norms, in addition to the imitation of behavior, that links domestic violence to juvenile delinquency.

DIFFERENTIALLY ASSOCIATING WITH DOMESTIC VIOLENCE

The data reported in the previous section also lends support to the theory of differential association. Much social learning takes place in one's intimate personal groups. Thus, behavior is learned by association with the behavior regardless of the morality of the person teaching (Sutherland and Cressey 1970, 75–81). The child learns violent behaviors through association both as an observer and as a recipient of violence within the home. Theoretically, the greater the association with domestic violence, the more likely violent behaviors will be learned without respect to the child's evaluation of the parent figure's evaluation of the parent figure's morality and norms. A second point can be made in relation to differential association. Many children flee abusive homes by repeatedly running away (Kempe and Kempe 1978, 42; Smith, Berkman, and Fraser 1980, 141–43). Escape behaviors such as runaway and drug or alcohol abuse are frequently in reaction to abuse in the home. Bolton, Reich, and Gutierres (1977) and Gutierres and Reich (1981) report that abused children are more likely to engage in escape instead of aggressive behaviors. Sutherland and Cressey (1970, 212–13) note that the unpleasant home forces the child out, which "is likely to increase the child's association with delinquency behavior patterns and decrease his association with anti-delinquency behavior patterns."

The study provides evidence of this association from the types of discipline experienced by respondents reporting runaway, drug use, and alcohol use. Of those experiencing physical and abusive discipline, 79.5% reported runaway, 89.5% drug use, and 91.2% alcohol use, while only 70.0%, 85.0%, and 85.0% respectively reported these behaviors for those not physically disciplined. These differences are small, but a consistent pattern indicates that the more abused juveniles more frequently reported involvement in the escape behaviors.

Responses to the question relating the juvenile's reactions to parental discipline provided stronger support. A total of 113 responses of runaway were recorded after parental discipline, and of these, 83.2% were in response to physical or abusive discipline. Additionally, 27 responses indicated drinking or drug use immediately following discipline, with 85.2% of these were in response to physical and abusive discipline. Domestic violence forces the juvenile out of the home into situations that may place them in association with delinquent behavior patterns.

Sutherland and Cressey (1970, 215) note that the behavior of delinquents differs from their nondelinquent siblings with the observation that "parental affection and supervision vary considerably in the home." The literature on child abuse frequently notes that a single child may be the target of abuse, even to the point of becoming the scapegoat of the entire family (Fontana 1976, 83). The juveniles in the sample seemed to perceive themselves in this role.

They repeatedly noted on the questionnaires that their siblings were treated differently, in a less physical manner. For a statistical example, 64.4% reported being slapped by their male parent figures, while only 25.7% of those with brothers and 31.9% with sisters reported observing their male parent slap the respective sibling. This type of difference was found for each kind of abusive behavior committed by both the male and female parent figures. Therefore, in the perception of the respondents, they were differentially associated with the physical discipline behaviors of their parents when compared to their siblings. Differential involvement in delinquency appears to be related to differences in experience with domestic violence.

SOME CONCLUDING REMARKS

This study has contributed to the evidence of a link between domestic violence and juvenile delinquency. Juveniles reporting the most extensive histories of experience and observation of domestic violence reported the greatest variety of participation in delinquency. The social control theory was offered to explain this link. Domestic violence may interfere with the development of the attachment and belief elements of bond. This would increase the probability of delinquency. Further, delinquent behaviors may be learned through imitation by those who experience or observe domestic violence. Successful behaviors, even violent ones, may be imitated, transmitting the behavior, but not the norms.

However, evidence was found that domestic violence leads to both aggressive and escape reactions by the victims. By running away, the juveniles may come into association with other delinquent youth and through this association learn additional delinquent behaviors.

A word of caution should be added. The study did not have a control group, the measure of delinquency was simplistic, and only the frequency and seriousness of parental discipline were measured. A control group, the frequency of delinquent behavior, and child neglect should be considered in further research. Different forms of neglect and abuse may have different effects on delinquency or operate by different causal processes. This has been suggested recently by Brown (1984, 271) who reported that delinquency was related to neglect and emotional abuse, but not to physical abuse. One may find that a home environment that is both violent and rejecting may have quite different effects than one that is only violent or only rejecting. Future studies should include all forms of maltreatment.

The use of domestic violence measures may have distinct advantages for the researcher in juvenile delinquency theory. One is that it can be purely a measure of behavior. This avoids subjective evaluations of parents' or childrens' attitudes toward each other or of their behavior. One needs only to establish the frequency of specific types of behavior experienced or observed within the home. Evaluations, such as calling some of the behaviors abusive, need not be made to examine the effects of behavior on behavior.

The second factor is that domestic violence may provide a measure that avoids or accounts for the effects of social class. Domestic violence is found in all social classes as a result of stresses upon families. Indeed, Brown (1984, 270) found maltreatment and delinquency to be related independent of the effects of social class. Stress and the ability to deal with it is distributed differently among the social classes with the lowest being the most stressed and least able to cope. Therefore, one should find domestic violence and juvenile delinquency to be similarly distributed. One would expect to find that environments that are both stressful and violent produce more delinquency than those in which nonviolent solutions to stress are found.

In relation to the administration of the juvenile justice system, one can refer to the recent issue of commingling abused children, status offenders, and serious juvenile delinquents (Smith Berkman, and Fraser 1980, 46–60, 66–68). Certainly, children taken into the custody of the state for reason of child abuse should not be housed with juvenile delinquents. However, the reverse is a situation that cannot be avoided. The weight of the evidence from this and other studies is that the majority of incarcerated juvenile delinquents are abused children. They are both victim and offender and demonstrate characteristics of both. Their delinquency may be a symptom of their victimization, not an indicator of their deviance. The number of the survey participants who were still actively in crisis from their severe physical and sexual abuse experiences was shocking. Yet, these children were being dealt with by society as delinquents without regard to their needs as victims.

Juvenile justice treatment programs must be able to deal with the aftereffects of their clients' victimization within the home. An awareness of the need for an interdisciplinary and interagency community team approach has been reached in both the juvenile justice and the child protective fields. Now it must be realized that this team approach should occur between these two major social systems. If domestic violence, juvenile delinquency, and adult criminality are not separate issues, but are instead interwoven, the social systems responding to these problems should be interwoven.

Society needs to provide such a coordinated response through an exchange of ideas, treatment models, information, and referrals to improve prevention and treatment efforts. Networking among agencies steps forward in providing this exchange. Until violence is viewed in a more unified manner by society's response systems and a coordinated community response is developed, much domestic violence will continue to be undetected and untreated and much delinquency will result.

REFERENCES

Alfaro, J. 1978. *Report on the relationship between child abuse and neglect and later socially deviant behavior.* Albany, N.Y.: New York State Assembly Committee on Child Abuse.

Bach-y-Rita, G., and A. Veno. 1974. Habitual violence: A profile of sixty-two men. *American Journal of Psychiatry* 131:1015–17.

Bandura, A., and R. H. Walters. 1958. Dependency conflicts and aggressive delinquents. *Journal of Social Issues* 14:52–65.

Bender, L., and F. Curran. 1940. Children and adolescents who kill. *Journal of Criminal Psychopathology* 1:297–322.

Bolton, F. G., J. Reich, and S. E. Gutierres. 1977. Delinquency patterns in maltreated children and siblings. *Victimology* 2:349–59.

Brown, S. E. 1984. Social class, child maltreatment, and delinquent behavior. *Criminology* 22:259–78.

Campbell, J. S. 1974. The family and violence. In *Violence in the family,* edited by S. Steinmetz and M. Straus. 251–61. New York: Harper and Row.

Corder, B. F., B. C. Ball, T. M. Haizlip, R. Rollins, and R. Beaumont. 1976. Adolescent parricide: A comparison with other adolescent murder. *American Journal of Psychiatry* 133:957–61.

Duncan, G. M., S. H. Franzier, E. M. Litin, A. M. Johnson, and A. J. Barron. 1958. Etiological factors in first-degree murder. *Journal of the American Medical Association* 168:1755–58.

Easson, W. M., and R. M. Steinhilber. 1961. Murderous aggression by children and adolescents. *Archives of General Psychiatry* 4:27–35.

Fontana, V. J. 1976. *Somewhere a child is crying.* New York: New American Library.

Grinnell, R. M., Jr., and C. A. Chambers. 1979. Broken homes and middle-class delinquency: A comparison. *Criminology* 17:395–400.

Gutierres, S. E., and J. W. Reich. 1981. A developmental perspective on runaway behavior: Its relationship to child abuse. *Child Welfare* 60:89–94.

Helfer, R. E., and C. H. Kemp. 1976. *Child abuse and neglect.* Cambridge, Mass.: Ballinger.

Hennessy, M., P. J. Richards, and R. A. Berk. 1978. Broken homes and middle class delinquency. *Criminology* 15:505–27.

Hirschi, T. 1971. *Causes of delinquency.* Berkeley, Calif.: University of California Press.

Justice, B., and R. Justice. 1976. *The abusing family.* New York: Human Sciences.

Kempe, R. S., and C. H. Kempe. 1978. *Child abuse.* Cambridge, Mass.: Harvard University Press.

Kratcoski, P. C., and L. D. Kratcoski. 1982. The relationship of victimization through child abuse to aggressive delinquent behavior. *Victimology* 7:199–203.

Langley, R., and R. C. Levy. 1977. *Wife beating: The silent crisis.* New York: Dutton.

Lewis, D. O., and S. S. Shanok. 1979. A comparison of the medical histories of incarcerated delinquent children and a matched sample of nondelinquent children. *Child Psychiatry and Human Development* 9:210.

McCord, J., and W. McCord. 1958. Effects of parental role model on criminality. *Journal of Social Issues* 14:66–75.

Nettler, G. 1974. *Explaining crime.* New York: McGraw-Hill.

Nye, F. I. 1958. *Family relationships and delinquent behavior.* New York: Wiley.

Oliver, J. E., and A. Taylor. 1971. Five generations of ill-treated children in one family pedigree. *British Journal of Psychiatry* 119:473–80.

O'Neill, J. A., Jr., W. F. Meacham, P. P. Griffin, and J. L. Sawyers. 1973. Patterns of injury in the battered child syndrome. *Journal of Trauma* 13:332–39.

Pemberton, D. A., and D. R. Benaday. 1973. Consciously rejected children. *British Journal of Psychiatry* 123:575–78.

Peterson, D. R., and W. C. Becker. 1965. Family interaction and delinquency. In *Juvenile Delinquency: Research and Theory*, edited by H. C. Quay. 63–99. New York: Van Nostrand.

Sargent, D. 1962. Children who kill: A family conspiracy? *Social Work* 7:34–42.

Scott, P. D. 1973. Fatal battered baby cases. *Medicine, Science, and the Law* 13:197–206.

Sears, R. R., E. E. Maccoby, and H. Levin. 1974. The sources of aggression in the home. In *Violence in the family,* edited by S. Steinmetz and M. Straus. 240–46. New York: Harper and Row.

Sendi, I. B., and P. G. Blomgren. 1975. A comparative study of predictive criteria in the predisposition of homicidal adolescents. *American Journal of Psychiatry* 132:423–27.

Smith, C. P., D. Berkman, and W. M. Fraser. 1980. *A preliminary national assessment of child abuse and neglect and the juvenile justice system: The shadows of distress.* United States Department of Justice, National Juvenile Justice Assessment Center. Washington, D.C.: USGPO.

Smith, S. M., and R. Hanson. 1975. Interpersonal relationships and child-rearing practices in 214 parents of battered children. *British Journal of Psychiatry* 127:513–25.

Sorrells, J. M. 1977. Kids who kill. *Crime and Delinquency* 23:312–20.

Steele, B. 1976. Violence within the family. *Child abuse and neglect: The family and the community*, edited by R. E. Helfer and C. H. Kempe. 3–24. Cambridge, Mass.: Ballinger.

Steinmetz, S. K. 1977a. The use of force for resolving family conflict: The training ground for abuse. *The Family Coordinator* 26:19–26.

——. 1977b. The cycle of violence. New York: Praeger.

Steinmetz, S. K., and M. A. Straus. 1974. Violence in the family. New York: Harper and Row.

Sutherland, E. H., and D. R. Cressey. 1970. *Criminology*. 8th ed. Philadelphia: Lippincott.

Tanay, E. 1973. Adolescents who kill parents: Reactive parricide. *Australian and New Zealand Journal of Psychiatry* 7:263–77.

7

Criminal Justice Students' Perceptions of Satanism: Debunking Myths

James B. Wells, Brian P. Nicoletti, and
Patricia R. Roerig

PREFACE

To investigate the manner and degree to which the use of a course aiding in dispelling any misconceptions that criminal justice students had in relation to the satanism crime myth, two primary statistical techniques were utilized to analyze the data gathered with the Satanism Perception Scale: Pearson's product-moment correlation and the Student's T-test. Pearson's r was used to determine the relationship between: (1) precourse satanism perception and estimates of crimes linked to satanism, and (2) precourse satanism perception and the perceived importance of factors believed to cause people to become involved in satanism. The T-test was used to examine differences in satanism perception means between the two different admininstrations of the Satanism Perception Scale. Furthermore, a paired samples T-test was utilized to examine if there was a significant decrease in student santanism perception after completing the course.

INTRODUCTION

One of the standard mechanisms for broadening an individual's intellectual scope, depth, vision, and understanding obtained from a liberal arts education is the debunking of myths (Durham 1992). As a result of all of the recent attention the media has given crime and justice issues, one of the most fertile issues for myth-debunking is criminal justice (Durham 1992). Many students in this country come to the university with perceptions toward crime and justice that "often are at considerable variance with reality, and not surprisingly, the judgments based upon these perceptions are often equally lacking in sensibility" (Durham 1992, 46). The following paper describes a mechanism by which criminal justice students had an opportunity to explore the myth-creation process as well as to learn how to exercise reasoned empirical judgment about important social issues. The mechanism used in one elective criminal justice course was student perceptions toward satanism.

Why has the practice and participation in satanic and occult activities attracted so much attention from the public and the criminal justice community? One of the main reasons can be directly traced to the lack of truly credible information on the subject. Information about satanism and the occult is often inconsistent, unreliable, misrepresented, and sometimes fabricated. Some Christian fundamentalists, political extremists, bereaved parents, opportunists, and mentally unstable individuals are promoting information on what is, by every independent investigation, a nonexistent problem (Alexander 1990). "In reality, what they offer is little more than fundamentalistic misdirected grief of bereaved parents, and the fantasies of self-seeking opportunists disguised and promoted as scholarship and criminology" (Alexander 1990, 5). Furthermore, no proof has been found that satanic-related crime exists on a scale that warrants new criminal laws and special task forces (Hicks 1991; Lanning 1992; Jenkins 1992).

While there is a wide assortment of pieces of information relating to satanism and occultism, very little of the information has any veracity. One possible explanation for the lack of accurate information could be that many academicians have considered satanism and the occult to be a topic unworthy of serious consideration. Furthermore, hardly anyone from the law enforcement community has tried to combat publicly the overstatements, generalizations, absurd facts, illogical reasoning, and so forth that some people have made about satanism and the occult (Hicks 1991). However, a growing number of social scientists are recommending that satanism and antisatanism warrant serious examination because this movement's influence now extends into important segments of American society (Richardson, Best, and Bromley 1991a). Whereas some credible and empirical research on the topic of satanism has recently begun to emerge (see especially Richardson, Best, and Bromley 1991b), it is doubtful that the majority of criminal justice students would consider expending the time and effort necessary to locate it on their own initiative. Today's criminal justice students need to be informed that they should exercise restraint and skepticism towards some of the things they may encounter in their profession, or else possibly face financial loss, as well as professional and public embarrassment. Already, evidence is emerging that unjustified crusades against those perceived as satanists is resulting in wasted resources, unwarranted damage to reputations, and disruption of civil liberties (Victor 1990).

The main objective of the study was to assess the effectiveness of a course designed to better inform criminal justice students about current crime myths, particularly those involving satanism and the occult. If students can have their perceptions altered by the introduction of empirical information on a very controversial subject, then they stand a greater chance of becoming better criminal justice practitioners. It is hoped that a college undergraduate degree in criminal justice will give students the proper tools to become more than just interested bystanders in the criminal justice field. Hopefully, this course, as well as others in the college curriculum, will motivate students to become more rigorous and demanding in their inquiries so that they will not be hindered by bias or by unsubstantiated information.

While most social research topics are well defined and investigated by scientists, the areas of satanism and occult activity are so new to the arena of social research that there are few real theories advanced on the subject. While the charges and accusations about satanism and occult-related crimes encompass all demographic borders, researchers have been hesitant in exploring this phenomenon.

One theory that has been proposed by Crouch and Damphousse (1991) is that the police are victims of misinformation in much the same way that the public is being misguided. In a study done by these researchers (1991), they developed and administered a Satanism Perception Scale. These surveys were sent to police officers who had shown some interest in occult crimes by attending one or more seminars identified by the researchers. Information obtained from their survey, along with evidence that true satanic crimes are very rare, led the researchers to believe that the officers were clinging to biased or religious views toward satanism and occult crimes. Apparently, limited, direct experience with serious occult crime and frequent exposure to lurid, unsubstantiated accounts about such crime elsewhere lead many officers to see satanism as a major national threat (Crouch and Damphousse 1991). With respect to lurid, unsubstantiated accounts of occult crime, Jenkins and Katkin—in their essay in Kappeler, Blumberg, and Potter's *The Mythology of Crime and Criminal Justice* (1993)—describe how the media has promoted sensationalist views and acted as accomplices in modern-day witch-hunts:

> On serial murder, satanism, child abuse, and abduction, the most reputable television shows presented quite outrageous fantasies as sober fact. When the McMartin story first made the news in early 1994, magazine programs like "20/20" treated the charges as automatically correct, with the children as victims of appalling treatment. (42)

In a content analysis of newspapers and their reporting of the antisatanism movement, Crouch and Damphousse (1992) concluded that newspapers promote a public perception of satanism by publishing especially lurid stories for economic gain and by providing a forum for satanism "experts" (e.g., police officers and religious leaders).

Hicks (1991) contends that a major source of misinformation is generated by the police themselves. Many of the cult experts are police officers who have attended occult training seminars and workshops devoted to the methods and practices of satanism and the occult. At these training seminars, news stories and unsubstantiated rumors are given credence by the speakers. The new trainees then go back to their departments with this new knowledge and spread it to others in their area of influence. They then become experts in their own right and are in turn interviewed by the media. This process turns out to be a vicious circle of flawed logic with each new printing of the same rumors being used to substantiate the same rumor.

These seminar trainees accept the information from these seminars as facts because they lack access to empirically based research. One source of empirical research comes from Richardson, Best, and Bromley, who edited the collection of essays *The Satanism Scare* (1991). In this book the scientific model of inquiry is applied to a diverse array of issues that include the perception, belief, practice, and investigation of the occult. Essays in this book offer a scholarly and professional opinion that find many of the claims about satanism implausible. An article by Jenkins (1992) that appeared in the *Police Forum* also suggests that the occult crime phenomenon has been "massively exaggerated" (1) and that any increased attention to this alleged form of activity may lead agencies to seek an "occult dimension" where in fact none exists. An entire book devoted to dispelling the myth and mystery that surround satanism and the occult is *In Pursuit of Satan* (1991) by Hicks. After first discussing what can be considered the beginning of the problem, Hicks investigates and dissects most of the claims put forward by the true believers in satanism. As more scientifically based research on satanism and the occult become more accessible, one hopes that the criminal justice profession will become better equipped to reach its own conclusions with regard to this myth. The present study attempted to identify, measure, and analyze those specific beliefs in satanism and occult-related crime both prior to and after the course. If these students are to be the criminal justice professionals of the future, it is noteworthy to identify and measure their change in perceptions due to education.

There were several limitations present in this study. First, the factor of time as a limitation was considered. The students could only undergo ten weeks of class. A second limiting factor was the number of students involved in the study. The course was taught at only one institution. The region of the institution and the predominant religious beliefs of the majority of the students were also considered as limitations. The region is rural and is located in southern Appalachia. Most students are from conservative, middle-class families that are Protestant in religious orientation. In the absence of any other information, these students have been very much influenced by their families and their churches, as well as the news media. While the course will try to dispel any mystery and falsehood surrounding satanism and occult practices, a lifetime of parental influence and religious teaching is hard to dislodge. The impracticality of a true random sample and control group was also considered a limitation to this study, since there was a limited number of students available for the course and subsequent testing. Being limited to a one-group pre-test/post-test design, the authors were unable to control for several possible threats to internal validity that could have become confounded with the effect of the treatment variable (i.e., the course).

RESEARCH DESIGN

The primary purpose of this study was to measure the perceptions of criminal justice students before and after a college-level course on the topic of satanism and the occult. It was hypothesized that if the course was successful in its purpose, the perceptions of the students should change to more skeptical views of ungrounded accusations of criminal activity regarding satanism and the occult.

Subjects

The subjects for this study were drawn from those students who were enrolled in three separate sections of the course over a two-year period (courses were not offered concurrently). A prerequisite for the course was that the student be a declared major in the Criminal Justice Program.

Research Measure

The instrument utilized for this study was an edited version of an instrument developed by Crouch and Damphousse at Texas A and M University (1991). Their instrument, entitled the "Satanism Perception Scale," was administered in questionnaire form to police officers. Information gained from their instrument was used primarily to describe how the police perceived relationships between satanism and crime.

The edited version used for this study deleted all questions directly related to the official functioning of a police officer and concentrated on the perception-based questions. Crouch and Damphousse (1991) utilized eight of the perception-based questions to measure general perceptions of the satanism problem. The scale is scored by assigning the numbers 1–5 to the choices allowed for each item, so that a high score indicates that satanism is a clear and present danger in need of immediate attention. Conversely, lower scores describe subjects who see satanism in much less threatening terms. For some items, agreement with the statement indicated that subjects viewed satanism as a threat; for others, disagreement indicated subjects viewed satanism as a threat (see Table 7.4 for the direction in which items were scored). Scores on all eight items are summed so that a total satanism perception score is calculated.

The pretest instrument was in a questionnaire format and was administered on the first day of the course. The instrument has simple instructions and is designed to be self-administered. Background and biographical information on the students were gathered utilizing another questionnaire administered to all of the students in the Criminal Justice Program. The completed questionnaires were placed in storage until the final grades for the course were turned into the Registrar's Office. Students were informed that the instructor would not have access to the completed questionnaires until after the final grades were turned in.

In their published article, Crouch and Damphousse reported that the intercorrelation between total "satanism perception" scale score and each of the eight component items ranged from .641 to .774. Since this instrument was the only one the present authors could identify as pertaining to criminal justice and perceptions of satanism and the occult, this study has utilized it also.

Treatment

The specific treatment was an elective, college-level criminal justice course taken for credit toward a Bachelor of Science in Criminal Justice. First, the course outlined the history of the major religions and historical figures that have significantly contributed to the occult and to satanic religions. During this part of the course, students were given the opportunity to observe that there are obvious parallels between modern-day satanism hysteria and the satanism hysteria that has occurred in the past (e.g., the Salem witch trials of the seventeenth century). Students learned that "subversion myths" often emerge throughout history whenever rumors claim that some type of alien group is threatening society. For example, subversion myths about witches, Jews, or communists have surfaced whenever people have felt that their traditional values were being threatened by social problems (Victor 1990). As a result of the increasing breakdown of the family structure, many parents today are seeking similar scapegoats for their fears and frustrations (Victor 1990).

The course then described both pro and con views toward a satanism/occultism link with criminality, by first presenting material, literature, and media examples that suggested that satanism is a serious problem worthy of governmental intervention. For example, antisatanism literature was read and videos were seen that described public declarations made by alleged satanic cult participants and victims who survived horrifying experiences, including ritual torture and sexual abuse. In this part of the course, students observed that the rash, unsubstantiated claims that some people make about satanism have the effect of inciting public hysteria. Students also observed that many innocent people are themselves victimized whenever they make appeals to the scapegoating frenzy (Victor 1990). The latter part of the course emphasized a model of critical and empirical thought in relation to the specific claims of occult experts and "cultcops," ritual-abuse survivor claims, and satanic-related crime. For example, when it was discussed in the course that many people, including some "cult cops," believe that just because two variables are correlated they can be assumed to be causally connected (e.g., heavymetal music and satanism), the instructor pointed out that correlation is only one of the three criteria required to establish causality. Another example would be the error of logic that some "cult cops" make when they rationalize the lack of evidence at a possible crime scene as proof of the existence of a highly sophisticated network of satanists. It is important to note that the theme of the later part of the course was not against the idea that satanism is linked with criminality. Rather, the theme was that students and criminal justice practitioners should view evidence with a critical and unbiased eye that is untainted with the prejudices of religion and personal feelings. As before, literature, videos, and other material were presented to the students supporting this view. Throughout the course, the instructor attempted to avoid any bias or prejudice by never revealing or expressing personal feelings regarding the existence of (an) anthropomorphic malevolent spirit(s). Information was simply presented to the students that either supported or contradicted the two themes of the course.

The post-test instrument was administered on the last day to all students who had completed the course and who had been given the pretest. The same written and verbal instructions for completion of the instrument were given by the instructor of the course.

DATA AND RESULTS

Of all of the students registered for the three separate sections of the course, 88% responded to the pretest on the first day of the course as well as the post-test on the last day of the course (n = 70). Students were primarily male (66%) and white (94%), with a mean age of twenty-three. About 70% considered themselves to come from families where the primary caregiver was a white collar worker; 64% indicated that they were most strongly affiliated with the republican party, 20% indicated democratic, and 10% indicated independent. With respect to religious preference, 67% were Protestant, 14% Catholic, and 19% other. About 53% of the students indicated that they attended church services at least once a month. Of these, 13% reported they attend once a month, 14% attend two to three times a month, 22% attend weekly, and 4% attend more than once a week.

One issue we were very interested in examining was the seriousness to which criminal justice students perceive satanism as a criminal threat. This question was considered important given the great assortment of opinions among criminal justice personnel as well as recent empirical evidence suggesting that it is not as correlated with crime as many, often self-proclaimed, experts suspect (Damphousse and Crouch 1992). Student estimations of the percent of selected crimes in the country attributable to satanism are provided in Table 7.1.

Although there were vast differences in the sample regarding the estimated percent of crimes linked to satanism, data indicate that students perceive eleven in one hundred homicides, almost half of all animal mutilations, about one in five missing children and illegal drug use incidents, about eighteen in one hundred child abuse incidents and sex crimes, and one in fourteen suicides to be satanism related. These results suggest that criminal justice students do indeed regard satanism as a serious crime problem.

Table 7-1 Student Estimates of Percent of Selected Crimes in America Attributable to Satanism in the Past Year.

Crime	Mean Percent Estimated to be Satanism Influenced %	Standard Deviation
Homicide	11.56	12.00
Animal Mutilations	45.06	30.13
Missing Children	20.00	21.24
Child Abuse	18.66	20.69
Sex Crimes	17.93	15.79
Illegal Drug Use	20.53	20.51
Teen Suicide	25.26	20.76

To determine whether there is a relationship to student estimates of satanic influence on crime and antisatanist attitudes, we correlated crime estimates to the pretest eight item Satanism Perception Scale scores (see Table 7.2). Because of the possibility that the relationship between crime estimates and satanism perception scores might be curvilinear, we inspected bivariate scatterplots. For all crimes estimates, the path of the data points were approximately linear.

Table 7.2 reveals that the higher students score on the Satanism Perception Scale, the more they are likely to believe criminal activity is influenced by satanism. Criminal activity significantly related to Satanism Perception Scale scores include homicide ($r = .403$, $p < .001$), missing children ($r = .375$, $p < .001$), and sex crimes ($r = .293$, $p < .01$). These correlates suggest that when students contemplate a relationship between satanism and crime, they may be associating their knowledge of "ritualistic crime" with their antisatanist attitudes. This association would be consistent with the emphasis of much of the antisatanist literature and media coverage describing how satanic ritual crime consists of child kidnappings, sexual abuse, and human sacrifice.

To explore relationships between student perceptions of satanism prior to the course and factors that students believe

Table 7-2 Correlation Matrix of Pretest Satanism Perception Scale Score and Estimates of Percent of Crimes Linked to Satanism.

	1	2	3	4	5	6	7	8
1. Satanism Perception	1							
2. Homicide	.403**	1						
3. Animal Mutilations	.178	.270	1					
4. Missing Children	.375**	.415**	.359**	1				
5. Child Abuse	.240	.496**	.292*	.539**	1			
6. Sex Crimes	.293*	.573**	.289*	.362**	.648**	1		
7. Illegal Drug Use	.192	.353*	.222	.185	.378**	.578**	1	
8. Teen Suicide	.250	.503**	.446**	.289*	.380**	.625**	.460**	1

* p < .01.
** p < .001.

Table 7–3 Correlation Matrix of Pretest Satanism Perception Scale Score and Importance of Factors Believed to Cause People to Become Involved in Satanism.

	1	2	3	4	5	6
1. Satanism Perception	1	.385**	.276	.438**	.284**	.431**
2. Heavy Metal Music		1	.827**	.654**	.089	.245
3. Music Videos			1	.553**	.046	.163
4. Fantasy Games				1	.033	.348**
5. Drug Usage					1	.554**
6. Moral Values Breakdown						1

* $p < .01$.
** $p < .001$.

cause people to become involved in satanism, we correlated pretest Satanism Perception Scale scores with several "causal factors" also measured by Crouch and Damphousse's instrument (see Table 7.3). Bivariate scatterplots between satanism perception scores and causal factors revealed the path of data points to be approximately linear.

As indicated by Table 7.3, the more the students viewed these factors to be influential in causing people to become involved in satanism, the higher they scored on the Satanism Perception Scale. Positive and significant correlations were found with all of the factors except "music videos." This pattern is consistent with much of the antisatanist literature and mass media the general public comes into contact with describing how fantasy games, breakdown of moral values, heavy metal music, and drugs (Bromley 1991) are causing young people to be drawn to satanism. Interestingly, the correlation between Satanism Perception Scale score and music videos was weakest and nonsignificant, indicating, perhaps, that the students are already familiar with the content of most music videos and realize that they are not a primary causal factor in drawing people to satanism. Although some of these factors were significantly correlated with satanism perception, the shared variance accounted for by the strongest correlation (r = .438) accounted for only 19.2%.

Next we looked at the relationships between pretest Satanism Perception Scale scores to three personal characteristics of the students: age, year in college, and church attendance. Age (r = −.087) and year in college (r = −.042) were not significantly correlated. Only church attendance was found to be significantly related to Satanism Perception Scale score (r = .3657, p < .001), suggesting that active involvement in a church is an important factor in antisatanism perception among students.

We turn now to the primary concern of this study: to what extent can a course aid in dispelling any misconceptions that criminal justice students have in relation to satanism and satanic-related crime? We direct our attention now to comparing students perceptions toward satanism prior to the course with those perceptions after the course by utilizing the eight-item Satanism Perception Scale.

Reliability estimates using Cronbach's coefficient alpha yielded the following reliability coefficients for the eight items in the Satanism Perception Scale: .85 for the pretest and .81 for the post-test. These reliability indices compare well with those reported earlier by Crouch and Damphousse (1991).

As expected, student perceptions prior to the course were that satanism is a clear and present danger in need of immediate attention. Table 7.4 presents the means and standard deviations for each of the eight items of the Satanism Perception Scale by pretest/post-test.

For each of the items in the satanism scale, there was a noticeable change in mean score after the course was taken.

With respect to the pretest and post-test differences in total Satanism Perception Scale score, Table 7.5 presents the means and standard deviations by pretest/post-test.

As expected, the higher scores were on the pretest Satanism Perception Scale, indicating that prior to the course, respondents were likely to perceive satanism as a clear and present danger in need of immediate attention. After the course, the satanism

Table 7–4 Satanism Perception Item Scores by Pretest/Post-test.

Item	Direction Scored	(Pretest)		(Post-test)	
		Mean	S.D.	Mean	S.D.
1. Satanism is morally wrong	+	4.09	.94	2.84	1.27
2. Most teenage dabbling in satanism and the occult is harmless	−	2.34	1.06	3.24	.99
3. Special legislation to deal with occult practices is not necessary	−	2.43	.97	3.81	.91
4. We should use any means available to stop the spread of of satanism in this country	+	3.34	1.10	1.97	.83
5. Actually, satanic activity is not a threat to society	−	2.43	1.07	3.70	1.20
6. Satanism and the occult could become as much of a problem as drugs in this country	+	3.34	1.03	2.27	.95
7. Sometimes I think there is a secret, organized effort to promote and protect satanism in America	+	2.71	.87	1.90	.80
8. Satanism is not as serious a problem as some people would have have you believe	−	2.67	1.02	4.01	.80

Table 7–5 Satanism Perception Scale Scores by Pretest/Post-test.

Satanism Perception Scale	N	Mean	S.D.
Pretest	70	27.61	5.68
Post-test	70	18.39	5.13

Table 7–6 Satanism Perception Item Responses by Pretest/Post-test.

Item	Strongly Disagree %	Disagree %	Undecided %	Agree %	Strongly Agree %
(1) Satanism is morally wrong					
pretest	00.0	8.6	14.3	37.1	40.0
post-test	12.9	37.1	15.7	21.4	12.9
(2) Most teenage dabbling in satanism and the occult is harmless					
pretest	21.4	41.4	22.9	10.0	4.3
post-test	1.4	31.4	12.9	50.0	4.3
(3) Special legislation to deal with occult practices is not necessary					
pretest	12.9	50.0	21.4	12.9	2.9
post-test	00.0	14.3	8.6	58.6	18.6
(4) We should use any means available to stop the spread of satanism in this country					
pretest	2.9	24.3	24.3	32.9	15.7
post-test	31.4	44.3	20.0	4.3	00.0
(5) Actually, satanic activity is not a threat to society					
pretest	24.3	25.7	35.7	11.4	2.9
post-test	1.4	11.4	22.9	50.0	14.3
(6) Satanism and the occult could become as much of a problem as drugs in this country					
pretest	1.4	24.3	25.7	35.7	12.9
post-test	17.1	54.3	14.3	12.9	1.4

Table 7-6 (*continued*)

Item	Strongly Disagree %	Disagree %	Undecided %	Agree %	Strongly Agree %
(7) Sometimes I think there is a secret, organized effort to promote and protect satanism in America					
pretest	4.3	40.0	38.6	14.3	2.9
post-test	31.4	52.9	10.0	5.7	0.0
(8) Satanism is not as serious a problem as some people would have you believe					
pretest	14.3	27.1	38.6	17.1	2.9
post-test	00.0	8.6	4.3	64.3	22.9

perception scores dropped approximately 9 points, implying that satanism is much less likely to be perceived as a threat. A paired samples T-test revealed that there was a significant decrease for pretest to post-test in satanism perception scores ($t = 15.34$, $df = 69$, $p < .0001$).

Closer examination of pretest and post-test changes in the choices of the scale in Table 7.6 illustrates the extent perceptions changed.

Very surprising is that prior to the course, 62.9% of the students disagreed with the statement that "special legislation to deal with occult practices is not necessary." However, after the course, only 14.3% of the students disagreed. Another dramatic change occurred with the statement that "we should use any means available to stop the spread of satanism in this country." Prior to the course, almost half (48.6%) of the students agreed with the statement. However, only 4.3% agreed with the statement after the course. Changes in the perceived seriousness of the satanism problem are also quite striking, with only 20% of the students agreeing with

Item 8 (seriousness of satanism) before the course, compared with over 87% of the students after the course.

CONCLUSIONS AND RECOMMENDATIONS

The perception that satanism may be connected to crime has become an important concern for many in the criminal justice community. However, few academicians have considered satanism to be a topic worthy of serious consideration in the criminal justice classroom, despite the fact that the misconceptions many people have about the satanism and crime relationship has resulted in squandered taxpayer dollars and public and professional embarrassment. Yet, since a growing number of social scientists are recommending that the criminal justice system's preoccupation with satanism warrants serious examination, we believe criminal justice students need to be instructed that they should exercise some restraint and skepticism if and when they are confronted with satanism in their professional career. The central concern of this study was to investigate the manner and degree to which the use of a course aided in dispelling any misconceptions that criminal justice students had in relation to satanism. Our inquiry suggests several conclusions and recommendations.

First, many criminal justice students believe that a large percentage of some selected crimes are linked to satanism. Since one of the main objectives of any college-level criminal justice program should be to educate students about the actual nature and extent of crime, we believe that misconceptions students have about the satanic crime myth, or for that matter, any type of crime myth, should be addressed at some point in a program's curriculum. Since crime myths emerge when social science fails to address certain questions (Kappeler, Blumberg, and Potter 1993), students need to be provided with the knowledge that crime myths can be addressed, treated, and analyzed.

Second, the belief that many students have about crimes being significantly influenced by satanism can be related to their antisatanist attitudes. Too many law enforcement officials have already transformed their legal duties into a moral confrontation between Christianity and the Devil. "Faith, not logic and reason, governs the religious beliefs of most people" (Lanning 1989, 62). As a result, some normally skeptical police officials accept information about satanism without critically evaluating it (Lanning 1989). If those in powerful positions accept the reality of the satanism scare, then basic legal rights and protections for everyone may break down. As criminal justice educators, our job is to teach our students how to enforce the law, not their own morality or religious beliefs.

Finally, results from this study indicate that the students had different perceptions and attitudes at the end of the course than they had at the beginning. Although limitations of the research design do not allow us to claim with any conclusive proof that it was the course that changed attitudes, we do believe that the experience was not only successful in training criminal justice students to view information on satanism through a more unbiased and critical eye, but also in fostering a more objective and analytical approach to any criminal justice related information. Many students mentioned that they viewed the course as an important link and a real-life application of the concepts and processes learned in not only the "investigative techniques" course offered at the college, but also in the "social science research methods" course that is offered. For example, students in the course came to realize that the police investigator and the social science researcher assume very similar responsibilities. To illustrate, both the police investigator and social science researcher examine evidence, sift and weigh the facts, formulate hypotheses, search for evidence that both supports and refutes the hypotheses, and so on. Or, in other words, both the investigator and the researcher engage in deduction and induction!

We believe that other criminal justice instructors should give this topic as well as other current crime myths the attention they deserve at some point in their program's or institution's curriculum. Some predict that the satanism panic will become an even larger growth industry in the 1990s (Alexander 1991). Since many people, including public leaders as well as criminal justice officials, take the claims about the criminal link of satanism and the occult seriously, we suggest that criminal justice scholars do so as well.

REFERENCES

Alexander, D. 1990. Giving the devil more than his due. *The Humanist* 50(2):5–15.

———. 1991. Still giving the devil more than his due. *The Humanist* 51(5): 22–33, 42.

Bromley, D. 1991. Satanism: The new cult scare. In *The satanism scare*, edited by J. Richardson, J. Best, and D. Bromley. 49–72. New York: Aldine De Gruyter.

Crouch, B., and K. Damphousse. 1991. Law enforcement and the satanic crime connection: A survey of "cult cops." In *The satanism scare*, edited by J. Richardson, J. Best, and D. Bromley. 191–204. New York: Aldine De Gruyter.

———. 1992. Newspapers and the antisatanism movement: A content analysis. *Sociological Spectrum* 12(1):1–20.

Damphousse, K., and B. Crouch. 1992. Did the devil make them do it? An examination of the etiology of satanism among juvenile delinquents. *Youth and Society* 24(2):204–27.

Durham, A. M. 1992. Observations on the future of criminal justice education: Legitimating the discipline and serving the general university population. *Journal of Criminal Justice Education* 3(1):35–51.

Hicks, R. D. 1991. *In pursuit of Satan: The police and the occult.* New York: Prometheus Books.

Jenkins, P. 1992. Investigating occult and ritual crime: A case for caution. *Police Forum* 1(January):1–7.

Jenkins, P., and D. Katkin. 1993. Protecting victims of child sexual abuse: A case for caution. In *The mythology of crime and criminal justice*, edited by V. Kappeler, M. Blumberg, and G. Potter. 37–51. Prospect Heights, IL: Waveland Press.

Kappeler, V., M. Blumberg, and G. Potter. 1993. *The mythology of crime and criminal justice.* Prospect Heights, IL: Waveland.

Lanning, K. 1989. Satanic, occult, ritualistic crime: A law enforcement perspective. *Police Chief* 56(10, October):62–85.

——. 1992. *Investigators guide to allegations of "ritual" child abuse.* Quantico, Virginia: National Center for the Analysis of Violent Crime, Federal Bureau of Investigation.

Richardson, J., J. Best, and D. Bromley. 1991a. Satanism as a social problem. In *The satanism scare*, edited by J. Richardson, J. Best, and D. Bromley. 3–17. New York: Aldine De Gruyter.

——, eds. 1991b. *The satanism scare.* New York: Aldine De Gruyter.

Victor, J. S. 1990. The spread of satanic-cult rumors. *Skeptical Inquirer* 14(3):287–91.

8

Regression Analysis Applied to Local Correctional Systems

Randall Guynes and Tom McEwen

PREFACE

Unlike many of the other articles in this text where a particular statistical technique was used to analyze data in an attempt to examine some research question, this article demonstrates how a statistical technique can be used to help solve or predict information necessary to make policy decisions. In this case, regression analysis is used to supply necessary information about daily jail populations in an effort to assist in expansion needs.

As part of a project conducted in 1991 for the Montgomery County, Maryland, Council of Government, the authors conducted univariate and multivariate regression analysis on several important influences on the County's criminal justice system: crimes, arrests, average daily jail population, and persons under correctional control. The analysis of crimes and arrests included Part I classifications (homicide, rape, robbery, assault, burglary, larceny, and auto theft), and Part II classifications (examples include simple assault, disorderly conduct, offenses by juveniles, narcotics violations, vandalism, and others). The intent was to model these overall categories against key socio-demographic characteristics over a twenty-one-year period. The variable on average daily jail population is defined as the average number of persons who are in jail on any given day, and the last variable on persons under correctional control combines persons incarcerated in the County jail with those assigned to several alternative programs. The overall aim of this portion of the study was to determine whether the County's jail facility needed to be expanded and, if so, what size it should be to accommodate the County's needs into the next century.

THE SETTING

At the time of the study, the County operated the Montgomery County Detention Center (MCDC) as its primary jail. Defendants sentenced by District or Circuit Court judges to less than one year of incarceration must serve their time in Montgomery County's facilities. For offenders sentenced from one year to eighteen months, Maryland law allows the sentencing judge to decide whether the person will be incarcerated locally or at a state facility. However, overcrowding at the state level has put pressure on judges to keep offenders locally. Of course, the MCDC also houses pretrial defendants pending their court actions.

In July 1986, a renovation of the MCDC resulted in an addition of 72 single cells for men and 56 single cells for women, increasing the amount of bed space from 166 to 294 beds. However, even as these sections opened, the inmate population exceeded the increased bed space, on average, by 160 beds per day. The ADP of the facility increased from 290 inmates in 1980 to 640 inmates as of January 1, 1991. These increases alarmed the County government and led to studies, described below, on the future needs for correctional facilities and alternative programs.

An arrested or incarcerated person could shorten his/her jail incarceration time through three County efforts. These are the Pretrial Services Unit, the Pre-Release Center, and the Community

Accountability, Reintegration, and Treatment (CART) program. For the current study, the importance of these programs is that they reduce the average daily population in the jail and reduce the number of cells needed in the future. Each program, however, has its own maximum capacity, which can limit the growth and extent to which it can be used.

The County implemented the Pretrial Services Unit (PTSU) in October 1990 as a program to supply information to the judges to determine whether selected low-risk pretrial defendants can be released from incarceration. PTSU staff conduct assessments of defendants and present the results to the judge, often accompanied by a specific release recommendation. It uses ten general screening criteria to assess a defendant's release risk, including such factors as length of residence, family ties, employment status, prior criminal record, physical and mental condition, and financial resources. The unit also tracks and supervises defendants who come under their control through the judge's decision.

The County's Pre-Release Center (PRC) is designed to facilitate community reintegration of offenders who are nearing the end of their periods of incarceration. It is a 120-bed residential facility consisting of one 32-bed coed unit and two 44-bed male units. The program primarily serves offenders who are County residents with short-term sentences (up to eighteen months). Participants must be within six months of potential release, have no serious pending court charges, no revocations from a work-release program (in the last two years), and be physically and psychologically capable of performing in the PRC program.

By way of background, two earlier studies had projected quite large numbers for future jail capacity. One study, completed in 1988, projected an average daily population of 1,700 persons by the year 2010, using a straight-line projection of average daily population figures. Because the County experienced a significant increase in jail population during 1988, another study was performed to modify the earlier projections taking into account the sudden jail population increase. The second study's projections for the year 2010 for average daily population amounted to 2,440 persons—a 43% increase over the earlier study. These projections meant that the County would have to significantly increase the size of the jail. Options were considered, but never enacted, to expand the current facility or to build a new facility at another location. At an estimated cost of $75,000 per cell, the projections could be met only through substantial costs to the County's taxpayers.

As experience began to show, however, both studies were incorrect. The jail population dropped off dramatically in 1990, down to levels experienced in 1987. While exact reasons for the downturn are debatable, two factors seemed to emerge. First, the jail population was inflated by a heavy push to clean up open-air sales of drugs. As the police strategy became increasingly successful, the number of arrests dropped. Further, the entire criminal justice community worked to keep the jail population down. A number of initiatives began to bear fruit in late 1990, as the CART and PTSU became fully operational.

In July 1990, the Montgomery County Council approved initial design funds for a new detention facility, but did not believe the earlier jail-space projections were sufficient planning tools. Therefore, in October 1990, the Montgomery County government, through a competitive bid process, selected the Institute for Law and Justice to conduct a comprehensive analysis and projections study on the sizing of a new detention center.

Results from the study will be presented in the remainder of this chapter. The primary intent, however, is to illustrate the role that regression analysis can play in modeling key variables that have an impact on a jurisdiction's criminal justice system. The focus is, therefore, on selection of variables for a regression, interpretation of regression results, and policy implications from the analysis. We present three separate and independent analyses in the following sections to illustrate that regression analysis can provide insights into the correctional needs of a jurisdiction.

CRIME AND COUNTY POPULATION

Crime and arrest data were available from the County for 1970 through 1990, a twenty-one-year period. Both sets of data were further divided into Part I and Part II crime categories. Part I crimes are comprised of homicide, rape, robbery, assault, burglary, larceny, and auto theft. Part II crimes are less serious offenses including, for example, simple assaults, disorderly conduct, juvenile offenses, narcotics offenses, vandalism, and other minor offenses.

The approach taken for this section of the analyses was to perform regressions using County population as the independent variable against crimes and arrests as dependent variables. Figure 8.1 shows County population, total reported crime (Part I and Part II crime), and total arrests over the twenty-one-year period. The data points have been smoothed with a three-year average, because our interest is in the trends for these series, and the smoothing process facilitates the removal of random fluctuations in the annual data. As reflected in the exhibit, crime and arrests generally have increased along with population. That is, the County has experienced population increases over the twenty-one-year period, and these increases apparently have created opportunities for more crimes and, subsequently, more arrests.

Table 8.1 shows the results of simple linear regressions with smoothed population as the independent variable against reported crime and arrests (smoothed) as dependent variables. In these regressions, b_0 is the constant for the regression equation and b_1 is the coefficient for the population in thousands. For example, the regression equation for estimating Part I crimes is given by:

$$\text{Part I Crimes} = 1,810.7 + 38.3 * \text{Population in thousands}$$

This equation indicates that the number of Part I crimes increases at the rate of about 38 crimes per thousand population. The R^2-value of .50 means that about half of the variance for Part I crimes is explained by this equation, and the correlation between population and Part I crimes is therefore about .71 (the square root of the R^2-value).

The other regression equations show R^2-values ranging from .29 for Part II events to .60 for total arrests. In the case of total

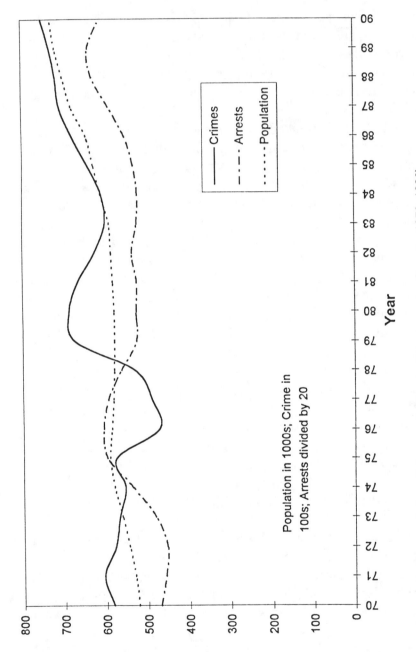

Figure 8.1 Population, Crime, and Arrests (Montgomery County, 1970–1990).

arrests, the value means that 60% of the variance in total arrests can be explained by the single variable of population. This result is fairly good in social science research where individual variables seldom account for major portions of a phenomenon. It is especially beneficial in the current context because arrests drive the jail's average daily population and total number of persons under correctional control.

The two prior studies also used annual data for their straight-line projections with *year* as the independent variable. The advantage of this independent variable lies with its simplicity, because data on other socio-demographic variables, such as population, do not have to be collected, with the *year* variable serving as a surrogate. Indeed, Figure 8.1 shows that increases in crime and arrests are somewhat linear over time. A straight-line regression will therefore yield statistically significant results. The disadvantage of this approach is that crime and arrests cannot be expected to increase at the same rate in future years and forecasts with year as the independent variable therefore eventually result in unrealistic estimates. Population is a better candidate in this regard, because of its natural causal connection with crime and arrests. While the County has enjoyed population increases over the years under study, its population will eventually level, and at that point, linear increases in crime and arrests will no longer apply.

Table 8–1 Regressions of Country Population against Crime and Arrests in Montgomery County, 1970–1990.

Variable	b_0	b_1	R^2	F	Sig F
Part I Crimes	1,810.7	38.3	.50	18.7	.000
Part II Crimes	3,029.4	56.4	.29	7.8	.012
Total Crimes	4,840.1	94.7	.50	18.6	.000
Part I Arrests	3,177.5	2.6	.40	12.6	.002
Part II Arrests	−1,059.8	11.9	.47	16.9	.001
Total Arrests	2,117.7	14.6	.60	28.0	.000

Table 8-2 Correlations among Socio-Demographic Variables, Montgomery County, 1970–1990.

Variable	Number of Households	Persons Employed	Percent White School Enrollment	Total School Enrollment	Unemployment Rate
County Population	.96	.94	−.90	−.54	.34
Households	1.00	.99	−.98	−.75	.53
Persons Employed		1.00	−.99	−.79	.56
Percent White School Enrollment			1.00	.84	−.62
Total School Enrollment				1.00	−.84

A correlation analysis was conducted with other demographic variables to determine if improvements might be possible over the Table 8.1 results. As indicated in Table 8.2, relatively high correlations exist among the demographic variables. In fact, very high correlations are prevalent between the variables for population, number of households, number of persons employed, and the percent of white school enrollment. Forcing these variables into a regression would not provide significant improvements because of the multicollinearity reflected by these variables. After taking population into account, the other variables do not contribute to the regression because they provide redundant information.

Reasonably high correlations can also be seen between these variables and the two remaining variables of total school enrollment and unemployment rate. These variables also appear to provide redundant information because of their relatively high correlations. In fact, in a stepwise regression using these variables and total arrests as the dependent variable, County population was the only variable selected for the equation.

In summary, the univariate regression analysis performed for this study indicates that the County can develop reasonably good estimates for future crime and arrests by simply tracking population. Including other variables into the analysis will not improve significantly on the modeling of these variables.

An advantage of this result is that the professional staff in the County responsible for planning have been especially active in tracking and monitoring the County's growth. They have performed several studies on what could be expected in the way of population growth, households, businesses, and overall land use. Their studies served as the foundation for determining the expansion of a range of County services, including park services, fire suppression, police, and others. Their estimates on population have proven over time to be very accurate. As a result, the County was in a good position to take advantage of the regression approach in obtaining estimates on future crime and arrests.

EXTERNAL FACTORS AND AVERAGE DAILY POPULATION

The next analysis was on modeling the average daily number of persons under correctional control. Two different variables will be discussed in this section: average daily population (ADP) in a jail and total average daily population under correctional control. The latter term refers to the persons in the jail and under the control of the alternative programs of PTSU, CART, and PRC. By combining these groups, we gain more stability over time and improve the chances for successful modeling.

Before presenting the analysis, it is important to understand what the term *average daily population*, or ADP, means in correctional literature. In a jail setting, the ADP is calculated by first determining the total jail person-days for a time period, usually a month or a year, and then dividing by the number of days. A person who spends 21 days in jail contributes that number of person-days to the total during the time period. If a jail experiences 94,000 person-days during a year, then the ADP is 257.5 persons per day (94,000 divided by 365). Thus, ADP is simply the number of persons that we expect to see, on average, each day in the jail. The *actual* daily population will usually differ from this average number on any given day. It may be higher on Mondays because of arrests over the weekend and even higher during the summer months when police departments tend to make more arrests. These fluctuations are important because the size of the jail facility cannot be based solely on the average, but must be large enough to handle these fluctuations.

The ADP for the total population under correction control simply expands the ADP definition to incorporate those under control through the PTSU, CART, and PRC alternatives. Because data on the alternatives were available only since 1978, we based our analysis on the thirteen-year period from 1978 to 1990. For Montgomery County, this ADP increased steadily from 309 in 1987 to 724 in 1988. It then jumped significantly in 1989 to an ADP of 874 persons before dropping again in 1990 to an ADP of 762 persons.

As with crime and arrests, County population turns out to be a good estimator for the ADP under correctional control. For the years under study, a correlation of .933 was obtained between ADP and population. The R^2-value for the univariate regression equation is therefore .870, which means that about 87% of the variance in ADP can be explained by the population variable. The resulting regression equation was as follows:

$$ADP = -1,169.3 + 27.28 * \text{Population in ten-thousands}$$

The equation can be viewed as saying that each increase in County population of 10,000 residents will result in an estimated increase of about 27 persons under correctional control on a daily basis. The standard error of the estimate for ADP was calculated to be 63.2 persons, which theoretically means that for 95% of the data points, the estimated value will be within 1.96 times 63.2, or 124, of the actual value.

Figure 8.2 shows the actual ADP for the years under consideration along with the regression estimates, including upper and lower limits based on the mean square error. The regression line is a smooth curve moving through the actual ADP figures. The

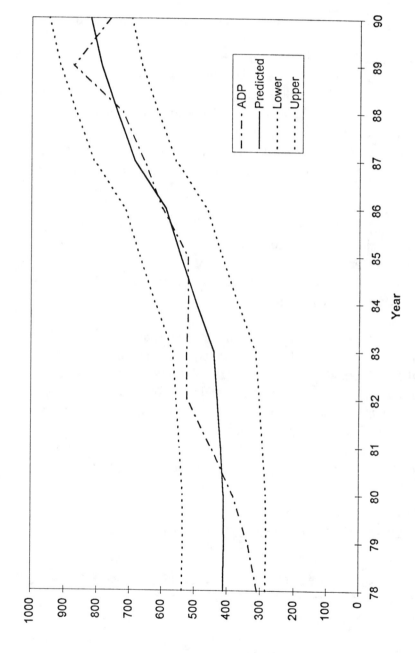

Figure 8.2 County Population and ADP.

exhibit shows that all the actual ADP points are between the lower and upper bound. In fact, ten of the thirteen data points are within one standard error of the estimate.

The ADP analysis can be applied in a very practical way to determine jail sizing as defined by the amount of bed space that the County will need in the years after 1990. Suppose that the County planners estimate that the County's population can be expected to continue to increase at about 3% per year as it has done for the past few years. This information can be used to estimate the number of beds for the correctional facility based on the results of the regression analysis.

Table 8.3 shows the estimates made for jail sizing assuming a 3% population growth factor. The estimates for the capacities of the alternative programs (PTSU, PRC, and CART) were developed in a separate report based on an analysis of staffing levels, physical space, financial requirements, and other factors for these programs.

In Table 8.3, the first column is the year and the second column is the estimate of ADP under correctional control from the regression equation. The next three columns are estimates of the ADP for the three alternative programs based on the separate analysis previously mentioned. These alternative program estimates are then subtracted from the regression estimate to obtain the "MCDC" column. As discussed, the estimates need to take into account that the daily population will vary on any given day

Table 8-3 Jail-Sizing Projections for Montgomery County, 1991–1995.

Year	Regression Estimate	PTSU	PRC	CART	MCDC	Safety Factor	Beds Needed
1991	897	49	140	64	644	124	768
1992	920	51	144	66	659	124	783
1993	943	52	147	67	677	124	801
1994	966	53	151	69	693	124	817
1995	1,000	55	156	71	718	124	842

because of seasonal influences (e.g., more arrests during the summer), daily influences (e.g., more arrests on weekends), and random fluctuations. To be sure that enough beds are available for these variations, a *safety factor* is calculated as 1.95 times the standard error. This factor is then added to the MCDC total to give the last column, which is the estimated number of beds.

These projections could, of course, be extended for more years than shown in the exhibit. However, several limitations begin to emerge in extending the estimates. We based the regression on thirteen years of data—a good rule of thumb is not to predict beyond about half the number of data points. The estimates for the alternate programs are also problematic for future years. At the time of the study, the PTSU and CART programs had been in operation for only a couple of years, and estimates on their success and growth in future years are tentative at best.

The regression analysis nevertheless served as an excellent tool for the County to determine its jail-sizing needs. Compared to the prior studies, it provides a better theoretical foundation through selection of population as the independent variable. Moreover, it gives a relatively easy tool for County planners to revisit the correctional needs as time passes and to consider the effects of diversion programs.

INTERNAL FACTORS AND AVERAGE DAILY POPULATION

The analysis so far has looked at the effects of external factors, as reflected by population growth, on the ADP under correctional control. The analysis has ignored the fact that internal factors—especially policy decisions within the criminal justice system—can have an impact on average daily population. The aim in this section is to indicate some relationships between these internal factors and the ADP of a correctional system.

Before giving the main part of the analysis, we need to take a side trip to look at another variable that we call *jail intake*. Jail intake during a particular month is the number of people booked into the jail during the month. It differs from ADP because it measures *persons* rather than *person days*. For example, a jail might book 250 people during the month of April who stay in jail for an average of 6 days each. The jail intake is therefore 8.3 people per day (250 divided by 30) and the ADP for jail population is 50 people (250 times 6 divided by 30 days).

Jail intake is clearly a function of arrests made by the police. Using *monthly* data from 1984 through 1989 (72 months), we performed a stepwise regression using individual arrest categories as independent variables. The analysis showed that three variables were important in modeling jail intake:

Jail Intake = 84.5 + .449 * Part I Arrests + .816 * Part II Narcotic Arrests + .652 * Part II Other Arrests

This regression yielded a multiple R^2 of .80 and a standard error of the estimate of 45.70. The three variables therefore explain about 80% of the variance in monthly-intake levels.

While the relationship is strong by normal standards in social science analysis, it is a relationship that we see as problematic because of the selection of narcotics arrests during the stepwise procedure. We have every reason to believe that narcotic arrests will decrease in the long-term. On the other hand, we can conjecture that some other "crime priority" will replace drugs as a law enforcement thrust. Consequently, the use of the above equation for long-term projections is not advised because of the likely changes in policy on law enforcement strategies. The result is nevertheless interesting, because it clearly shows that drug arrests were a driving force during jail intake in the latter half of the 1980s.

Rather than considering jail intake as a dependent variable, we found that it had usefulness as an independent variable along with several other internal factors for estimating ADP for the jail. These factors were reflected in data provided by the County that included the totals by month for 1994 through 1989 on the following eleven variables:

Monthly jail intake

Number awaiting trial in District Court less than 90 days

Number awaiting trial in District Court 90 days or longer

Number awaiting trial in Circuit Court less than 90 days

Number awaiting trial in Circuit Court 90 days or longer

Number sentenced by the District Court for less than 90 days

Number sentenced by the District Court for 90 to 364 days

Number sentenced by the District Court for 365 days or more

Number sentenced by the Circuit Court for less than 90 days

Number sentenced by the Circuit Court for 90 to 364 days

Number sentenced by the Circuit Court for 365 days or more

In addition, several dummy variables were developed to indicate changes in jail capacity and the introduction of police "jump out" squads.[1] A stepwise regression was performed with ADP as the dependent variable and independent variables consisting of the eleven variables listed above and the dummy variables. In a very rare event in social science statistics, nine of the eleven variables from the list were selected by the stepwise procedure as statistically significant. Only circuit court sentences greater than one year and sentences less than 90 days did not add to the explanation of ADP. None of the dummy variables was found to be significant. Table 8.4 shows the regression coefficients from the stepwise multiple regression and Figure 8.3 shows the actual and modeled ADP over the seventy-two-month period. The exhibit clearly shows that the variables from the stepwise selection process capture the internal criminal justice factors on jail population.

The variables in Table 8.4 are listed in the order of jail intake, followed by four pretrial variables, and then four sentencing variables. The multiple R2-value is .97, which means that 97% of the variation in ADP is explained by these nine variables, and the standard error of the estimate was 24.52. As seen in Table 8.4, all variables are significant at the .05 level.

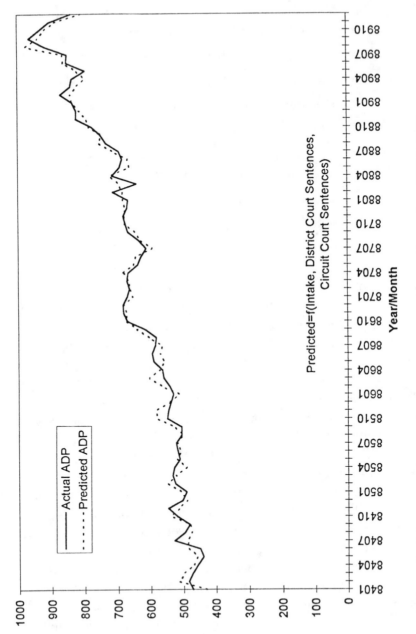

Figure 8.3 Average Daily Population (Montgomery County Corrections) (1984–1989).

Table 8–4 Stepwise Multiple Regression for ADP, Montgomery County, 1984–1989 Monthly Data.

Variable	Regression Coefficient	Standard Error of Coefficient
Constant	63.21	25.27*
Jail Intake	.22	.06**
Pretrial Variables		
District Court Pretrial Less than 90 days	.75	.13**
Circuit Court Pretrial Less than 90 days	.95	.16**
District Court Pretrial Greater than 90 days	.51	.16**
Circuit Court Pretrial Greater than 90 days	.79	.12**
Sentencing Variables		
District Court Sentence Less than 90 days	1.38	.40**
Circuit Court Sentence 90 to 364 days	2.07	.20**
District Court Sentence 90 to 364 days	.91	.32**
District Court Sentence Greater than 1 year	−1.31	.45*

* 5% level of significance.
** 1% level of significance.

One reaction to the approach in this analysis might be that the variable "jail intake" is tautological because it is logically related to ADP. While there is clearly a relationship between the two variables, the ADP for the jail is certainly not directly proportional to jail intake. Inmates stay in jail for varying amounts of time because of their status (pretrial versus sentenced), type of offense, and other factors. The interesting feature of the analysis, as previously indicated, is that eight other variables are statistically significant beyond jail intake. From a statistical viewpoint, therefore, jail intake is not the only factor of importance in explaining average daily population.

The coefficients in Table 8.4 measure the impact of the respective variables while controlling for the effects of all others. Consequently, in this particular application, interpreting the relationships among the individual coefficients can be tricky and often open to more than one interpretation. For example, we suspect that the two variables for pretrial less than 90 days reflect the impact of the previous two to three months of jail intake. The two variables for pretrial greater than 90 days may reflect the degree to which cases are taking longer to process. Court administrators would probably like these latter coefficients (on longer case processing) to have smaller coefficients than the coefficients on shorter case processing. Indeed, Figure 8.3 shows this conjecture to be the case for the respective courts.

The coefficients for the sentencing variables also provide insight into the relative strengths of the effects of the different sentences on ADP. It is apparent that the greatest relative impact is from circuit court sentences between 90 and 364 day—a result suggesting that the circuit court used these medium-length sentences during times of jail expansion. By contrast, the district court appears to have pushed its sentencing toward the use of shorter sentences, as reflected by relatively high coefficients for the two variables on district court sentences less than 90 days and between 90 and 364 days. The relatively high negative coefficient for district court sentences greater than one year suggests that the court has decreased its use of long sentences during periods of jail expansion.

CONCLUSION

The intent in this chapter has been to show that regression analysis can play a role in modeling average daily population and in determining jail-sizing needs for the future. The analysis included the impact of alternative programs on ADP and jail size, which are especially important practical considerations given the costs of new cell construction. Alternatives are important, because in identifying defendants of low risk, they allow jail resources to be used more effectively for defendants of higher risk. Other alternatives toward the end of incarceration assist by integrating inmates back into society with a higher probability of success. Freeing cells is an important by-product of these programs.

The analysis in this chapter shows that regression is beneficial in two other ways. First, it shows that changes in crime and arrests are associated in general fashion with changes in the County's population. This result supports the need for the County's planners to track population growth carefully as an indicator of impacts on the local criminal justice system. In other jurisdictions, this relationship may not hold true, especially when the jurisdiction's population level has stabilized, but crime fluctuates. Analysis needs to be conducted on a case-by-case basis to determine the key influencing factors in a particular jurisdiction. Second, the multiple regression analyses show that several factors internal to the criminal justice system are useful in modeling the ADP of a correctional system. These results could be beneficial to a court system if there is interest in helping to control ADP, as well as to legislators who want to be aware of the impact of sentencing legislation on a local correctional system.

---

1 "Jump out" squads were squads of officers who conducted street-level drug enforcement by converging on a location (such as a street corner), jumping out of their patrol cars, and arresting the drug sellers and buyers.

9

Community Policing in the Eye of the Beholder: Perceptions of the Community-Oriented Model

Allan Y. Jiao

PREFACE

Multiple regression is considered an especially important tool for social scientists in the analysis of nonexperimental data. Each of the two data sets analyzed in this paper was either originally a randomized survey sample, or used as such for the purpose of testing our research assumptions. Multiple regression is helpful in testing assumptions about a relationship between a set of independent variables and a dependent variable. In this study, two relationships are examined to help us better understand community policing. In testing relationships, multiple regression requires that choices of variables to be included in the statistical models be guided by theoretical considerations. We theorize that the two different sets of variables are related to the dependent variables, and we demonstrate that those particular variables have been well established in current police literature.

Although it is assumed that the effects of independent variables are additive and that the relationships being examined are linear, ordinal level variables and dichotomous variables can be used in multiple regression. In large samples we can rely on the Central Limit Theorem to ensure normal distribution in the population and conduct significance tests. Although problems may occur in multiple regression when two or more predictor variables are highly interrelated, the presence of multicolleniarity can be detected by observing dramatic changes in the size of coefficient estimates when we switch samples, change the indicators used to measure a variable in the model, or delete or add a variable to the equation.

Community policing has been criticized as a "cart-before-the-horse" movement (Rosenbaum, Yeh, and Wilkinson 1994), because it has usually been implemented without knowing how people perceive and understand the concept, nor the principles and activities associated with this policing approach. Community policing programs have also often been evaluated prematurely without due consideration of the length of time needed for a policing approach to take hold. Not surprisingly, most of these evaluations turned out to be negative about their findings (Jiao 1995a). In this paper, we focus on understanding people's perceptions of community policing and its effectiveness by using both first and secondhand data. It is believed that this understanding will serve as an important step for creating an effective community policing program. Once empirically demonstrated, the variables conducive to community policing and its effectiveness can be made known to concerned police departments. The two specific research questions this study will answer are: what perceptive variables support community policing that might be utilized or created by the police concerned? What community policing activities are regarded as more effective than others?

THE STUDIES

Data for our discussion of variables and activities contributing to community policing come from two sets of data collected in the city of Newark, New Jersey. The data from the author are a more general study of policing models conducted in May and June 1995 (referred to as The Police Model Study hereafter). The data from Pate and Annan (1993) are an evaluation of the effect of community policing programs on fear reduction conducted in 1983 and 1984 (The Fear Reduction Study, hereafter).

The Police Model Study

Respondents of this study were selected in a randomized survey from the urban center of Newark, including both community members and police officers. The "community member" in this case refers to an adult citizen who is related to the survey area by either residence, work, or business. Since the downtown district has more businesses than residences, a diverse and heterogeneous group of community members with different business ties to the area formed the majority of respondents to this survey. The major factors or variables specifically explored in this study include crime concerns, community consciousness, perceptions of important police activities, attitude toward the police, and constructs of community policing orientation. Besides thirty-four police officers who patrol the local community and participated in this study, probability samples were drawn from the business and residential community. In total, 575 questionnaires were distributed personally and 432 questionnaires were returned. Due to a large number of missing values in 63 questionnaires, 369 questionnaires were actually used for analysis. So the actual response rate for this survey is 64%. Only data related to respondents' demographic conditions and perceptions of community policing were used for this analysis, since the purpose of this article is to understand what variables are related to community policing.

The Fear Reduction Study

Several neighborhoods in Newark were surveyed in order to determine community policing activities and assess citizen attitudes towards the police. Baseline data were collected to determine citizen perception of crime, crime avoidance behavior, and citizen satisfaction with the quality of life in the neighborhoods. In addition, experiments were conducted to evaluate the effectiveness of special police programs designed to reduce the fear of crime within communities. The data were not analyzed as an experiment in this paper, however, because the purpose here is not to evaluate the effectiveness of community policing programs in Newark—that has been done elsewhere (Williams and Pate 1987) —but to examine the possible relationship of safety perceptions and different police activities with community satisfaction of life.

THE MODELS

In modeling a socio-political perceptive, a researcher often finds him- or herself in a difficult situation trying to determine what items to include to represent a particular model (Bohigian 1977; Lachman and McLauchlan 1977). Using too many items would reduce a model to an illustration; extreme brevity would render a model incomplete. A balance of the two is desirable but difficult. In this study, only those police activities and organizational principles relevant to the survey respondents and applicable to this urban community are selected. Police activities not typically conducted by the police under study are excluded. To build a statistical model for analysis, it is also necessary to justify the rationale behind the selection of those variables to be included. Community policing is based on a set of theoretical assumptions, organizational principles, and characteristic activities that should be incorporated into the model.

We build two different multiple regression models to serve our purposes with the two data sets. We use the Police Model data to test the effects of demographic and perceptive variables on community policing orientation (Model 1). The Fear Reduction data are used to assess the effects of safety perceptions and police activities on community satisfaction of life (Model 2).

Model 1

The dependent variable for the first model is "community policing orientation," which is derived from respondents' ratings from 1 to

6 (1 = strongly disagree and 6 = strongly agree) of two general statements, that is, "The police would be more effective if various community members were more involved in police operations," and "The police should develop a balanced and cooperative police-community program against crimes in the area."

The first model is tested by two multivariate regression analyses in order to ascertain whether demographic and perceptive variables are stable under different model conditions. In the first case, it was assumed that socio-economic background has a stronger effect on one's preference for community policing and thus includes eleven socio-economic variables (see Table 9.1, Model 1A). In the second case, it was assumed that perceptive variables have a greater effect on one's community policing orientation and thus decrease the number of demographic variables to three (see Table 9.2, Model 1B). Since community policing is a new approach, perceptions of this approach may have a stronger effect than do respondents' demographic variables.

Social class is included because community policing is regarded as an approach that empowers poor communities and bridges the gap between underclass communities and the police. As far as race is concerned, Asian, Hispanic, and American Indians are grouped as a single variable, because these minority groups have traditionally relied on an informal social control culture that is more consistent with the community approach. In contrast, Caucasians have a stronger individualistic tradition that might cause them to have lower agreement with the community orientation. "African-American" is the reference group for the race variable to avoid multicollinearity. Community membership is a variable that divides the sample into community and police. Since the police are trained mainly in accordance with professional principles, we believe that the community expects more community policing than the police officers do.

Since community policing is seen as an approach that will contribute significantly to the security of local residents and businesses due to its geographic focus, it is assumed that people with a higher stake in the community, such as business owners and

Table 9–1 Variables Used in the Multivariate Analysis of Community
Orientation (Model 1A).

Independent Variable	Measurement
I. Social-economic variables	
(1) Social class	5-level ordinal scale from "lower class" to "upper class"
(2) Being business owners/ residents	Binary, Respondents who are business owners or residents in the survey area versus those who are not
(3) Residential distance	4-level ordinal scale from "far from campus" to "on campus"
(4) Hispanic/Asian/American Indian	Binary, Respondents who belong to this racial category versus those who do not
(5) Caucasian	Binary: 1 = Caucasian; 0 = Not Caucasian
(6) Education	10-level ordinal scale ranging from "high school" to "Ph.D."
(7) Marriage	Binary: 1 = married; 0 = not married
(8) Children	Binary: 1 = have children; 0 = do not have children
(9) Age	Years
(10) Security guards	Binary, Respondents who are security officers versus those who are not
(11) Business employees	Binary, Respondents who belong to this status group versus those who do not
II. Perceptive Variables	
(12) Sense of community	3-level ordinal scale from "not a community" to "a community"
(13) Call the local police station	4-level ordinal scale from "call the local police last" to "call the local police first"
(14) Police service	5-level ordinal scale from "poor" to "excellent"
(15) Crime rate	5-level ordinal scale from "dropped dramatically" to "increased dramatically"
(16) Create/maintain good police-community relations	3-level ordinal scale from "no importance" to "great importance"

Table 9–1 (*continued*)

Independent Variable	Measurement
(17) Police role as community officers	4-level ordinal scale, range = "least important" to "most important"
(18) Community role as partner to the police	4-level ordinal scale from "least important' to "most important"
(19) Community participation	4-level ordinal scale from "least important" to "most important"

Table 9–2 Variables Used in the Multivariate Analysis of Community Orientation (Model 1B).

Independent Variable	Measurement
I. Socio-economic variables	
(1) Community membership	Binary: 1 = Community; 0 = Others
(2) Residential distance	4-level ordinal scale from "far from campus" to "on campus"
(3) Marriage	Binary: 1 = married; 0 = not married
II. Perceptive variables	
(4) Sense of community	3-level ordinal scale from "not a community" to "a community"
(5) Creat/maintain good police-community relations	3-level ordinal scale from "no emphasis" to "great emphasis"
(6) Foot patrol	3-level ordinal scale from "no emphasis" to "great emphasis"
(7) Meet community members	3-level ordinal scale from "no emphasis" to 'great emphasis"
(8) Talk to community members	3-level ordinal scale from "no emphasis" to "great emphasis"
(9) More problem solving	4-level ordinal scale from "strongly disagree" to "strongly agree"
(10) Police role as community officers	4-level ordinal scale from "least important" to "most important"
(11) Community role as partner to the police	4-level ordinal scale from "least important" to "most important"
(12) Community participation	4-level ordinal scale from "least important" to "most important"

residents in the area, are more receptive of community policing. Residential distance from the survey area is related to community policing, because the closer a respondent's residence to the community, the higher his or her stake in that community and, thus, community orientation.

Higher education is believed to be associated with community policing because this orientation represents an approach that encourages skepticism of what the police have always been doing, and emphasizes openness, communication, and innovation. Higher education and community policing are also considered as related because they both focus on the liberal social dimension of the police science.

Respondents who are married and/or have children tend to have a stronger interest in their community because their status in the community is more stable compared to singles or people without children. Older age also means less mobility and may be positively related to community orientation. Business employees and security guards compared to college students and other transient groups have an interest in community orientation due to their work connections to the community.

To determine respondents' perceptions of community policing, it is first necessary to determine people's sense of community. The question that solicits this information about the survey area includes three choices: (1) It is a not a community because there is no common purpose and no interaction among different community groups; (2) It is a community, but with only little common purpose and interaction among different community groups; and (3) It is a community, with both common purpose and interaction among different community groups.

The basic premise of community policing is that a community in fact exists or can be created. Community in its traditional sense means that people share a certain geographical area and have social interactions (Sullivan and Thompson 1990). This type of traditional community hardly exists in the modern American metropolis. Some researchers suggest that today's community can be viewed through the prism of issues such as crime, disorder, and fear that constitute the most urgent kind of community of interest

(Meenaghan 1972; Trojanowicz and Moore 1988). We therefore consider it appropriate to examine one's sense of community instead of the physical existence of community. Respondents' willingness to call the local police station instead of the police headquarters, their rating of the local crime rate and of the quality of police service, are other indicators that demonstrate and affect one's sense of community.

The five selected police activity variables perceived to be important are: creating and maintaining good relations between the police and the community; patrolling on foot and contacting community members regularly; meeting with various community groups to discuss community concerns; talking to community members for their help in obtaining possible crime evidence; and problem solving. The community policing approach recognizes that police are not able to reduce crimes only by improving internal management and by professionalizing themselves. Creating and maintaining good police-community relations is believed to have a direct impact on the community's ability to maintain stability and on the police department's capacity to deal with crime. Foot patrol is considered an important community policing activity that displays the principle of geographic focus and team policing. Police officers on foot patrol are believed best able to interact with community members and to develop good police-community relations (Fyfe 1985; Trojanowicz 1990). Community policing operations require police consultation with the public about what security needs are most pressing and the best way to go about meeting them cooperatively (Bayley 1994). Problem solving is considered an element of community policing, because this approach involves the community in defining and addressing various problems (Bayley 1994; Trojanowicz and Bucqueroux 1994). If perceptions of these activities are found to be positively related to community policing orientation, then the findings of this study can be interpreted as consistent with the theoretical assumptions and characteristic activities of community policing.

Perceptive variables also include perception of the role of the police and the role of the community. Community-oriented police agencies must broaden the scope of the police officers' roles and engage in proactive police activities. The community police officers must know the needs and preferences of community members and involve the community in policing. On the other hand, the role of the community need to be changed also. Community members who regard themselves as partners to the police and take seriously their participation in crime prevention will have an effect on both the community and crime. The fundamental principle of community policing is that community members must be involved in their own safety (Skolnick and Bayley 1988; Goldstein 1990; Sparrow, Moore, and Kennedy 1990; Trojanowicz 1990; Trojanowicz and Bucqueroux 1991 and 1994; and Cordner 1995).

Model 2

The second model selects variables from The Fear Reduction Study (see Table 9.3). To build the model, we first consider those variables that indicate reduction of fear of crime. We find that one's satisfaction with the quality of life and the quality of police services in a community to be a major indicator of reduced fear of crime. One's idea of whether the area one lives in has become better or worse is another important indicator of reduced fear. Thus we combine these two variables to create our dependent variable—satisfaction of life in the community.

Two sets of characteristics that reflect a respondent's likelihood of increasing his or her satisfaction of life in the community are examined. These are variables related to police activities and variables affecting respondents' own perceptions (see Table 9.3). We believe that one's satisfaction with community life is determined by both external and internal factors, thus we include these two kinds of variables in this model. Demographic variables have been excluded in this model because the purpose of this analysis is to study the effect of police-related variables and safety perceptions on community satisfaction of life, and also because demographic variables have been analyzed more appropriately in fear of crime studies (Marshall 1991; Covington and Taylor 1991; Keane 1992).

Table 9–3 Variables Used in the Multivariate Analysis of Community Satisfaction (Model 2).

Independent Variable	Measurement
I. Police activities:	
(1) Community meeting	Binary, Residents who attended meetings versus those who did not
(2) Rating of prevention	5-level ordinal scale from "very poor job" to "very good job"
(3) Increased police patrol	3-level ordinal scale from "decreased" to "increased"
(4) House protection	3-level ordinal scale from "not much safer" to "a lot safer"
(5) House inspection	Binary, Residents who received house inspection versus those who did not
(6) Pamphlets	Binary, Residents who received pamphlets verus those who did not
(7) Knowledge of Prevention	Binary, Residents who were aware of prevention versus those who were not
II. Residents' perceptions:	
(8) Safe at night	4-level ordinal scale from "very unsafe" to "very safe"
(9) Crime rate	3-level ordinal scale from "decreased" to "increased"
(10) Assault/robbery	3-level ordinal scale from "not worried" to "very worried"
(11) Drug-gangs	3-level ordinal scale from "no problem" to "big problem"

Three multivariate analyses were conducted to test the second model. In the first case (Model 2A), we draw variables reflecting community policing related activities that may increase a respondent's satisfaction of life in the community. These activities, which had been implemented by the police in Newark, include community meetings, crime prevention, increased patrol, household protection, household inspection, pamphlet distribution, and residents' awareness of police crime prevention programs (see first part of Table 9.3). Non-police-related activities are not included in the first analysis because of our focus on examining the "pure" effect of police-related variables.

In the second case (Model 2B), we draw some perceptive variables that may have an impact on respondents' satisfaction of life. We refer to these variables as internal, perceptive, or psychological variables, because they are related more to the residents' personal feelings and experience (see second part of Table 9.3). These variables have a strong tendency to exist regardless of police activities. They include residents' feelings of safety at night, perceived crime rate, their worry of being assaulted and robbed, and their concern with drug or gang problems. We seek the interaction effect between drug and gang problems and create the variable named "drug-gangs." We combine "worry of assault" and "worry of robbery" into one variable named "assault and robbery." Studying these internal psychological variables is important, because they can help us gauge their effect on community satisfaction of life in comparison to the effect of community policing activities.

In the third case (Model 2C), we examine the overall effect of both external and internal factors on increasing community satisfaction of life. Since one's happiness is affected by both objective and perceptive factors, the increase of happiness depends not only on whether the police are able to target crime problems appropriately, but also on whether the community's mentality can be changed by police activities.

ANALYSIS

The following analyses employ the technique of multiple regression, which enables the researcher to analyze virtually any set of quantitative data (Lewis-Beck 1980). Multiple regression analysis is considered an especially important tool for social scientists in the analysis of nonexperimental data (Berry and Feldman 1985). The Police Model Study is a cross-sectional survey. Although The Fear Reduction Study involves pre- and post-tests with both experimental and control samples, these data were not used here to evaluate the effectiveness of community policing in Newark. Rather, only the post-test data were used to compare the effects of police activities and safety perceptions on community satisfaction of life. As both data sets are examined as randomized survey samples, multiple regression is a natural choice.

Multiple regression helps us test our assumptions about a relationship between a set of independent variables and a dependent variable, since few phenomena are products of a single factor. In this study the correlation is tested by using demographic and perceptive variables as independent variables, and using community policing orientation as the dependent variable for The Police Model Study. The relationship between police activities and safety perceptions as independent variables, and community satisfaction of life as the dependent variable, is analyzed for The Fear Reduction Study. The effect of a particular independent variable is also made certain for the possibility of distorting influences from the other independent variables can be removed (Lewis-Beck 1985).

Multiple regression analysis must be guided by theoretical considerations in deciding which variables to include (Lewis-Beck 1980). "An investigator needs a sufficiently well-developed theory to know which variables should be in the equation and a set of indicators that measure those variables" (Berry and Feldman 1985, 25). As illustrated above, the variables we have included in our models are based on two theoretical considerations. First, we theorize in general that two different sets of variables have an impact on community orientation and satisfaction of life. Second, we demonstrate that those particular variables considered to be related to our dependent variables are well supported by the community policing literature.

In multiple regression analysis, we also assume that the relationship between the dependent variable and independent variables is linear, and that the effects of the independent variables are additive. As can be seen in our models, most of the variables are either ordinal or dichotomous instead of interval due to the nature of our study. However, "an ordinal variable is a candidate for regression, even though the distances between the categories are not exactly equal," and dichotomous variables can be modified and incorporated into the regression framework through the employment of dummy variables (Lewis-Beck 1980, 71).

We also need to assume normal distribution of the error term in the population for our multivariate analyses. In large samples, we can rely on the Central Limit Theorem to ensure that even if the error term is not normally distributed in the population, the sampling distribution of a partial slope coefficient estimator will be normally distributed (Hanushek and Jackson 1977). As Bohrnstedt and Carter (1971) have shown, regression analysis is quite robust against violations of normality and, thus, significance tests can be done in large samples even when this assumption cannot be justified substantively. Since The Fear Reduction Study is a fairly large sample (N of cases = 2653), we can safely rely on the central limit theorem. In contrast, the sample of The Police Model Study is much smaller, and statistical findings from it warrant more caution.

In a multiple regression analysis, the estimates of partial slope coefficients are, by definition, affected by the presence and absence of other variables. Entering a variable in a multiple regression equation, or deleting a variable, can have a major effect on the size of regression coefficients. A researcher runs into problems when two or more predictor variables are highly interrelated. The presence of multicollinearity can be detected by observing dramatic changes in the size of coefficient estimates when we switch samples, change the indicators used to measure a variable in the regression model, or delete or add a variable to the equation (Berry and Feldman 1985). This concern is one of the reasons why two data sets are used to test two models with different arrangements of variables. As can be seen in the following, there are no dramatic changes in the size of the coefficient estimates between the two analyses for Model 1 and the three analyses for Model 2.

RESULTS

Community policing orientation is tested with two different analyses. In the first case, despite nonsignificance of demographic variables, the model explains 23% of the variance associated with the dependent variable, the community policing orientation. The perception that it is important for the police to create and maintain good police-community relations, the perception that the

Table 9–4 Multivariate Analysis of Community Orientation (Model 1A).

Independent Variable	b	t
Intercept	1.704*	2.053
Socio-economic variables		
Social Class	−0.151	−1.475
Residents/business owners	0.249	0.560
Residential distance	0.104	1.457
Hispanic/Asian/American Indian	0.164	0.830
Caucasian	0.146	0.847
Education	−0.001	−0.043
Marriage	0.255	1.396
Children	−0.162	−0.815
Age	0.009	1.040
Security guards	−0.432	−1.267
Business employees	0.162	0.719
Perceptive variables		
Sense of community	0.182*	7.962
Call the local police	−0.054	−0.499
Police service	0.023	0.259
Crime rate	−0.090	−0.968
Create/maintain good police-community relations	0.476***	3.753
Police role as community officers	0.036	0.561
Community role as partner to the police	0.170*	20,288
Community participation	0.131	1.608

$R^2 = .23$.
$F = 2.621$, $P(F) < .0005$.
Degrees of freedom = 19,173.
* $p < .05$, *** $p < .0001$.

community should work as partner with the police, and one's sense of community are all significantly related to community-oriented policing (see Table 9.4).

In the second case, most of the demographic variables in Model 1A are eliminated in order to see if this arrangement will create any statistical significance among demographic variables. As can be seen in Table 9.5, these variables remain nonsignificant; and the R^2 for the model remains similar to the first analysis. Sense of community, perception of community as a partner with the police, perception of the importance of creating and maintaining good police-community relations, and preference for problem-solving activities are all significantly related to the community orientation. This result indicates that sense of community and

Table 9-5 Multivariate Analysis of Community Orientation (Model 1B).

Independent Variable	b	t
Intercept	0.928	1.461
Socio-economic variables		
Community membership	0.195	0.878
Residential distance	−0.033	−0.555
Marriage	−0.150	−1.118
Perceptive variables		
Sense of community	0.205*	2.319
Create/maintain good relations	0.313*	2.230
Foot patrol	0.089	0.644
Meet community members	0.103	0.825
Talk to community members	−0.081	−0.616
More problem solving	0.129**	2.920
Police role as community officers	0.049	0.807
Community role as partner	0.162*	2.298
Community participation	0.095	1.766

R Square = .21.
F = 4.209, P(F) < .001.
Degrees of freedom = 12,187.
* $p < .05$, ** $p < .01$.

Table 9–6 Multivariate Analysis of Professional
Orientation.

Independent Variable	b	t
Intercept	4.836***	7.748
Annual Income	0.032	0.996
Being male	0.034	0.193
Being police officers	−0.010	−0.027
Being Caucasian	0.486**	2.691
Years of age	−0.005	−0.443
Higher education	−0.169***	−5.174
Professional occupation	0.221*	1.958
Community orientation	0.085	1.410

$R^2 = .14$.
$F = 4.460$, P(F) $< .0001$.
Degrees of freedom = 8,238.
* $p < .05$, ** $p < .01$, *** $p < .0001$.

perception of what is important have a stronger effect on one's
community orientation than demographic conditions.

In order to answer the question whether the insignificance of
demographic variables is true also of other policing approaches
and is thus due to our sampling errors, we conducted a multivariate analysis using police professionalism as the dependent
variable. The result indicates significant effects of certain demographic variables (see Table 9.6). Caucasians, when compared to
minority groups, are more receptive of police professionalism.
Professional occupations compared to nonprofessional jobs are
also positively related to professionalism. Higher education, however, is negatively related to this policing approach. And the rating
of community orientation indicates that community policing is not
related to the professional approach. Therefore, it may be concluded that the community orientation is less affected by demographic variables.

The second model, which is based on the data of Pate and
Annan (1993) collected in 1983 and 1984 on reducing fear of

crime in Newark, is tested with three statistical analyses to assess the effects of community policing activities and safety perceptions on one's satisfaction of life in the community. The result of the first analysis (see Table 9.7, Model 2A) indicates that police activity variables have mixed effects on one's satisfaction of life. While community meetings, rating of police crime prevention, increased police patrol, and knowledge of prevention programs have significant and strong effects upon one's satisfaction, other activities like household inspection, household protection, and pamphlet distribution are not statistically significant. When these insignificant variables are excluded from analysis, the R^2 of .20 remains. This result shows that community members prefer some police activities to others. Community meetings, crime prevention, and increased police patrol require that the police really listen to the residents' concerns and that police officers and community members work together. These activities that are genuinely community-oriented and give a real impression of crime prevention on the residents have a statistically significant effect. Household inspection, household protection, and pamphlet distribution, on the

Table 9–7 Multivariate Analysis of Community Satisfaction by Police Activities (Model 2A).

Independent Variable	b	t
Intercept	2.822	22.896
Community meeting	0.229***	4.364
Rating of prevention	0.484***	21.559
Increased police patrol	0.144***	3.519
House protection	0.003	0.106
House inspection	−0.073	−0.550
Pamphlets	−0.030	−0.513
Knowledge of prevention	−0.763***	−4.060

R^2 = .20.
F = 90.427, P(F) < .0001.
Degrees of freedom = 7,2593.
* $p < .05$, ** $p < .01$, *** $p < .001$.

other hand, may only convey the rhetoric of community policing as far as the community residents are concerned.

It is also interesting to note in the first analysis that knowledge of prevention activities is significantly but negatively related to residents' satisfaction of life. This can be explained by the fact that those residents who were made aware of crime prevention programs were often informed at the same time about crime and security problems in the neighborhood. This information could create a more negative impression about the quality of life in the community than what residents had previously. This phenomenon is typical during the early stage of implementing community policing programs. Since community policing in Newark is one of the earliest community policing programs in the nation, this finding should not be considered abnormal.

In the second analysis (Model 2B), four internal psychological variables that may have an impact on increasing or decreasing residents' satisfaction of life are used. The result indicates that all these variables are significantly related to one's satisfaction of life (see Table 9.8). They produce an R^2 of .28, which indicates that a community member's personal perceptions about his or her community have a stronger effect on his/her community satisfaction level than the police activities do.

Table 9–8 Multivariate Analysis of Community Satisfaction by Perceptions (Model 2B).

Independent Variable	b	t
Intercept	7.070	65.645
Safety at night	0.082***	5.412
Crime rate	−0.774***	−21.934
Assault/robbery	−0.148***	−8.619
Drug-gangs	−0.002***	−7.585

$R^2 = .28$.
$F = 206.958$, $P(F) < .0001$.
Degrees of freedom = 4,2653.
*** $p < .001$.

Table 9–9 Multivariate Analysis of Community Satisfaction by Activities and Perceptions (Model 2C).

Independent Variable	b	t
Intercept	5.463	31.355
Activity variables		
Community meeting	0.120*	2.489
Rating of prevention	0.291***	12.937
Increased police patrol	0.062	1.657
House protection	0.025	0.833
House inspection	−0.006	−0.052
Pamphlets	−0.036	−0.682
Knowledge of prevention	−0.550***	−3.202
Perceptive variables		
Safety at night	0.054***	3.624
Crime rate	−0.643***	−17.926
Assault/robbery	−0.109***	−6.301
Drug-gangs	−0.001***	−4.962

$R^2 = .34$.
$F = 118.168$, $P(F) < .0001$.
Degrees of freedom = 11,2577.
* $p < .05$, *** $p < .001$.

The third analysis (Model 2C) examines the overall effect of police-related variables and perceptive factors on one's satisfaction of life. The combined effect with an R^2 of .34 increases the effect of police activity analysis by 14% and increases that of the internal perception analysis by only 6% (see Table 9.9). All four of the perceptive variables remain highly significant, while only two of the four significant activity variables remain the same. Variables related to residents' perceptions have a much more stable and stronger effect on satisfaction of community life.

DISCUSSION

The community policing and community satisfaction models provide a number of significant and important predictors of effective community policing effort. Perceptive variables have been found consistently in the two models to be more significant than the more objective variables, such as respondent demographics and police programmatic activities. Perception of an area as a community has a significant effect upon the community orientation. This relationship indicates that the stronger the sense of community, the more receptive the citizens will be of community-oriented policing. Community policing is, therefore, a policing approach that can be created and maintained if a strong sense of community can be created and maintained. Sense of community is a concept that has often been ignored in theoretical development and implementation of community policing. The police should try to mold and promote this sense of community if they intend to successfully implement community policing programs.

Community policing can be further understood by its distinction from professional policing in terms of the concept of community consciousness. Traditionally the police have relied on the professional orientation, which does not require the police to maintain a sense of community in their jurisdictions. This is because police professionalism focuses on internal police management and a sense of community becomes irrelevant to what the police do. Since police professionalism is independent of the citizens' sense of community, deliberate efforts to increase community consciousness will not affect citizens' support or lack of support for the professional approach. The opposite is true, however, of community-oriented policing.

As this study indicates, perception of the community's role as a partner with the police, perception of the importance of good police-community relations, and preference for more problem-solving activities are all significantly related to the community orientation. These elements of community perceptions should be considered invaluable police resources; they should be made full use of if they already exist and created if they do not through appropriate community police activities. The significance of all these perceptive variables indicates that one's perceptions have a stronger influence upon one's community policing orientation than one's demographic background, such as social class, community status, race, residence, marital status, education, occupation, and so on. It may imply that once the values of community policing are internalized, this policing approach can be implemented among any social strata or economic conditions. Therefore, it is important to understand that diverse socio-economic variables do not have to be obstacles in implementing community-oriented policing. The observation of Sherman (1987) that police efforts to involve citizens in policing are more successful in stable middle-class and lower-middle-class family neighborhoods than in transient, singles, apartment-building, or poverty-stricken neighborhoods need not be regarded as discouraging development of community policing programs in those areas. What is critical is whether a strong community value can be developed before and in the process of implementing community policing programs.

Developing stronger community values and more positive community perceptions may be the most serious challenge to the community policing effort. It is interesting to see that various community policing activities in Newark produced only a marginal effect at the time of the study compared to the effect of respondents' safety perceptions. The psychological effect with an R^2 of .28 had been established over a long period of time, while the effect of community policing programs with an R^2 of .20 may have been created due to the short-term community policing program. This analysis suggests that the police face more difficulty in targeting perceptive factors. This result is consistent with that of The Police Model Study in that perceptive variables are more significantly related to community policing orientation. Both academic researchers and community-oriented departments should give more attention to this question: how to cultivate stronger community values?

CONCLUSIONS

Careful analysis of community perceptions of a new policing approach can help the police better prepare for its implementation. In community policing, the police and active community organizations should first create and maintain a strong sense of community through community education, because community consciousness is significantly related to community policing and eventually to its success. It should also be understood that community policing is not a policing program, rather it represents a change in police culture and community values. Viewed from a larger sociopolitical perspective, community policing represents change toward a stronger informal social control system (Jiao 1995b). Simple and temporary police programmatic activities that do not touch upon the deep-rooted psychological perceptions among citizens will certainly not have an effect on social change, let alone create lasting community satisfaction and lower the crime rate. People who are eager to see the effect of a community policing program over a short period of time will certainly be disappointed.

REFERENCES

Bayley, D. H. 1994. *Police for the future*. New York: Oxford University Press.

Berry, W. D., and S. Feldman. 1985. *Multiple regression in practice*. Quantitative Applications in the Social Sciences. Newbury Park, CA: Sage Publications.

Bohigian, H. 1977. What is a model? In *Modeling the criminal justice system*, edited by S. S. Nagel. Beverly Hills, CA: Sage Publications.

Bohrnstedt, G. W., and T. M. Carter. 1971. Robustness in regression analysis. In *Sociological methodology*, edited by H. L. Costner. San Francisco: Jossey-Bass.

Cordner, G. 1995. Community policing: Elements and effects. *Police Forum*. Academy of Criminal Justice Sciences Police Section 5(3) July:1–8.

Covington, J., and R. B. Taylor. 1991. Fear of crime in urban residential neighborhoods: Implications of between- and within-neighborhood sources for current models. *The Sociological Quarterly* 32(2):231–49.

Fyfe, J. J. 1985. Introduction. In *Police management today: Issues and case studies*, edited by J. Fyfe. Washington, DC: International City Management Association.

Goldstein, H. 1990. *Problem-oriented policing*. New York: McGraw-Hill.

Hanushek, E. A., and J. E. Jackson. 1977. *Statistical methods for social scientists*. New York: Academic.

Jiao, A. Y. 1995a. Review of *The challenge of community policing: Testing the promises*, edited by D. P. Rosenbaum. *ACJS Today* XIV (3):20–21.

———. 1995b. Community policing and community mutuality: A comparative analysis of American and Chinese police reforms. *Police Studies* 18(3, 4): 69–91.

Keane, C. 1992. Fear of crime in Canada: An examination of concrete and formless fear of victimization. *Canadian Journal of Criminology*. 34(April):215–24.

Lachman, J. A., and W. P. McLauchlan. 1977. Models of plea bargaining. In *Modeling the criminal justice system*, edited by S. S. Nagel. Beverly Hills, CA: Sage Publications.

Lewis-Beck, M. S. 1980. *Applied regression: An introduction*. Quantitative Applications in the Social Sciences. Newbury Park, CA: Sage Publications.

Marshall, C. E. 1991. Fear of crime, community satisfaction, and self-protective measures: Perceptions from a midwestern city. *Journal of Crime and Justice* XIV (2):97–121.

Meenaghan, T. M. 1972. What means community? *Social Work* 17(6):94–98.

Pate, A. M., and S. Annan. 1993. Reducing fear of crime: Program evaluation surveys in Newark and Houston, 1983–1984. ICPSR 8496 in Inter-University Consortium for Political and Social Research, *Guide to Resources and Service 1992–1993*. Ann Arbor, MI: ICPSR.

Rosenbaum, D. P., S. Yeh, and D. L. Wilkinson. 1994. Impact of community policing on police personnel: A quasi-experimental test. *Crime and Delinquency* 50(3): 331–53.

Sherman, L. W. 1987. Policing communities: What works? In *Communities and crime*, edited by A. J. Reiss, Jr. and M. Tonry. Crime and Justice: A Review of Research, vol. 15. 159–230. Chicago: University of Chicago Press.

Skolnick, J., and D. H. Bayley. 1988. *Community policing: Issues and practices around the world*. Washington, DC: National Institute of Justice.

Sparrow, M. K., M. H. Moore, and D. M. Kennedy. 1990. *Beyond 911: A new era for policing*. New York: Basic Books.

Sullivan, T. J., and K. S. Thompson. 1990. *Sociology: Concepts, issues, and applications*. 2nd ed. New York: Macmillan.

Trojanowicz, R. 1990. Community policing is not police-community relations. *FBI Law Enforcement Bulletin*. 59(10):6–11.

Trojanowicz, R., and B. Bucqueroux. 1991. *Community policing and the challenge of diversity*. Community Policing Series, No. 21. Michigan: National Center for Community Policing, Michigan State University.

———. 1994. *Community policing: How to get started*. Cincinnati, OH: Anderson Publishing.

Trojanowicz, R., and M. Moore. 1988. *The meaning of community in community policing*. Community Policing Series, No. 15. Michigan: National Neighborhood Foot Patrol Center, School of Criminal Justice, Michigan State University.

Williams, H., and A. M. Pate. 1987. Returning to first principles: Reducing fear of crime in Newark. *Crime and Delinquency* 33(1): 53–70.

10

Examining Students' Perceptions of Policing and the Affect of Completing a Police-Related Course*

M. L. Dantzker and Nicky Ali-Jackson

PREFACE

Considering the nature of the research conducted, one of our main interests was to observe differences among perceptions of students at two different points in time. Since the Student's t allows us to compare means by groups, we employed this technique using the pair option. This allowed us to see what change, if any, had occurred for each perception statement and the scale, and whether the change was significant. To further determine whether factors such as gender and ethnicity, as well as time in and of itself, had any affect on the perceptions, a multiple analysis of variance (MANOVA) technique, known as a repeated measures analysis, was employed. This allowed

---

* This is a version of a paper presented at the annual conference of the Academy of Criminal Justice Sciences, Las Vegas, 1996.

us to look at whether time and gender and time and ethnicity were statistically significant to perceptions and the possible change.

There is little doubt that most people have an opinion of, attitude toward, or perception of policing or law enforcement and police officers. Public attitudes toward law enforcement officers have been examined over the past two decades (Carte 1973; Decker 1985; Glauser and Tullar 1985; O'Brien 1978; Walklate 1992). Attitudinal determinants often are drawn from perceptions of the police role, such as what society perceives as the primary goals of police, or whether patrol should be more proactive or reactive. While a societal controversy remains over duties of police, law enforcement agencies have maintained the necessity of either continuing or developing community policing programs. In addition, empirical literature on police-community relations continues to grow suggesting the importance of examining this issue (Alpert and Dunham 1986; Meagher 1985). Universities have even developed courses on police and community relations, using current textbooks available on this topic (Mayhill, Barker, and Hunter 1995; Radelet and Carter 1994).

Decker (1981) argues that "citizens are responsible for initiating police activity in the vast majority of criminal matters as well as the provisions of information useful in making arrests" (80). When citizens have negative attitudes toward police, they are more reluctant to approach and help them. To enhance police productivity, society must perceive law enforcement officers as competent and trustworthy. Thus, community perceptions of police clearly play a significant role in law enforcement practices and policies.

While research has been concerned with police-community relations, this study focused on college students' perceptions of police. Students are members of society, therefore, their attitudes, beliefs and perceptions often represent those of their communities. Studies have examined various factors contributing to citizens' attitudes toward police (CATP). Most studies have shown that CATP is mostly satisfactory (Murty, Roebuck, and Smith

1990). Scaglion and Condon (1980) found that actual personal contact with police officers in a positive manner had impact on public satisfaction. Their findings found no direct relationship between race, age, and income and positive perceptions. Yet, other studies have found that minorities and lower-income groups are generally more dissatisfied with their local police departments (Radelet 1987).

Despite the empirical contradictions, it is evident that the mass media has portrayed law enforcement in a negative manner. According to the 1991 Gallop Poll, 92% of Americans had either seen or read about the videotaped beating of Rodney King by Los Angeles police officers. This video, along with a host of other negative images flashed across American televisions, depicts police as brutal, racist, and, at times, out-of-control. Leff, Protess, and Brooks (1986) found that Chicago-area subjects exposed to a series of news reports on police-related issues, changed their attitudes toward police. Specifically, during the study period, one news channel reported numerous accounts of police brutality. After watching this series, subjects were more concerned with police issues than they had been prior to its broadcast.

These public images are also observed by American college students. Thus, this study hypothesized that at the beginning of the semester, students enrolled in law enforcement courses would have a negative attitude toward policing, yet at the conclusion of the class their perception of police would become more satisfactory.

With the growing number of criminal justice programs nationwide, and the increased student population majoring in the field, it is imperative to understand the impact our courses are having on these future employees of the system. Are educators helping to create a better image of our law enforcement system? As academicians, it is necessary to examine whether course content impacts our students.

This article reports the perceptions of students entering a police-related course and how those perceptions changed at the end of the course. Students are primarily criminal justice majors of various ethnicities, ages, and gender, whose employment goals range from law enforcement to practicing law. Measurement was accomplished through a twenty-item questionnaire given in a pre- and post-test manner to three sections of police courses offered at two different universities.

METHODOLOGY

Considering the exploratory nature of this research, "traditional" methodological techniques, such as using a previously tested questionnaire or random sampling, were not employed. Instead, a questionnaire designed specifically for this research was used. The questionnaire consisted of twenty statements about policing to which respondents indicated their level of agreement to the statement. A five-point Likert scale ranging from minus two (−2, extremely disagree) to plus two (+2, extremely agree) was used. The statements' contents were based on anecdotal and observational experiences of one of the researchers as a police officer, researcher, consultant, and college teacher. Twelve statements were written so that a positive perception required disagreement with the statement, while the remaining eight were written where a positive response indicated a positive perception. Overall, the more negative the mean values the stronger the positive perception.

The questionnaire was pretested during the Spring 1995 semester. Results indicated that no changes were required and that it measured what the researchers were interested in measuring. Employing face-validity responses were what were expected. An internal consistency analysis was conducted to determine if the twenty statements could be used as a scale. The findings indicated that fourteen of the twenty statements had high internal consistency, providing a scale we call Perception,[1] which had a Chronbach's Alpha of .80. Finally, in addition to the twenty statements, select demographic information was requested (see Appendix 10a).

A purposive sample of students was selected to participate. Questionnaires were distributed to all students in attendance the first day of specifically-selected criminal justice classes (Fall 1995) at two Chicago area universities: Loyola University (LU) (a private, Jesuit institution) and University of Illinois, Chicago (UIC) (a public, state-funded institution). At LU, students in two sections (one day and one night) of a course entitled "Municipal Police Operations," and at UIC, students in the course "Police in a Democratic Society" (one section) were surveyed. To examine the changes that may have occurred in the students' perceptions by the end of the semester, the questionnaire was redistributed during the last week of class. The data was coded and analyzed using SPSSPC+.

RESULTS

During the first stage of the data collection, among the three classes, 96 students completed questionnaires. At the end of the semester, 92 students completed questionnaires. Since we were interested in the change in perceptions over time, only those questionnaires that could be matched using a four-digit identifier supplied by the student, were ultimately used for the analyses. After eliminating unmatchable questionnaires, 83 cases were retained for analysis. Because females outnumbered males in the two Loyola classes, the gender distribution for the sample favored females (46 to 37; 55% to 44%). Ethnically, whites comprised 63% (n = 52); 63% (n = 52) of the sample were twenty-one years of age or younger; 69 (83%) were upperclass (juniors and seniors); 72 (87%) indicated that their major was Criminal Justice, and 24 (29%) advised that law enforcement was their employment goal (See Table 10.1).

Upon completion of the courses, the perceptions for all the statements changed, with 19 of the 20 being toward a more positive position. Only the mean for the statement regarding "giving officers more freedom" was more negative but was still, overall, a positive perception. However, despite the changes, only eight statements were statistically significant (p < .05): primary role,

Table 10–1 Sample Demographics (N = 83).

Variable	n/Percent
Gender	
Males	37 (44%)
Females	46 (55%)
Ethnicity	
White	52 (62%)
Af/Am	8 (10%)
Hispanic	16 (19%)
Other	7 (8%)
Age	
18	3 (4%)
19	12 (14%)
20	14 (17%)
21	23 (27%)
21+	29 (35%)
Year in College	
Soph	12 (14%)
Junior	32 (38%)
Senior	37 (44%)
Major	
Crim Just	72 (86%)
Other	9 (11%)
Employment Goal	
Law Enf	24 (29%)
Courts	4 (5%)
Correct	3 (4%)
Law	27 (32%)
Probat	3 (4%)
Other	12 (14%)

Note: Rounding or missing data account for some totals not equalling the N of 83.

level of competency, striking a minority, preventing crime, professionalism, benefit of the doubt, hesitate shooting, and drinking/drugs.[2]

With respect to primary role, this statement had the largest change. At the beginning of the semester, students were more agreeable that the primary role of police officers was crimefighter, but by the end of the semester, they were more disagreeable with this perception (m = .554 and m = −.458, respectively). For level of competency, students became more disagreeable indicating a better perception of officers as not being incompetent. This was also true for perceptions about striking minorities, preventing crime for whites, and whether officers should be counseled instead of fired for drinking or drug use. Students' perceptions became more agreeable about police acting as professionals, not hesitating in a shooting situation, and being given the benefit of the doubt. In

Table 10–2 T-test Comparison of Means Scores, by Time.

Variable	Mean (T1)	Mean (T2)	T-value
Primary role	.554	−.458	5.49*
Level of competency	−.747	−1.289	4.29*
Serve and protect	−1.000	−.800	−1.27
Corrupt act	−.598	−.390	−1.33
Strike a minority	−.171	−.500	2.37*
Ignore needs	−1.000	−1.060	.55
Preventing crime	−.476	−.951	2.97*
Harass or help	−1.374	−1.470	.96
Unknown reaction	.482	.716	−1.65
Professionalism	.183	.598	−3.38*
Help society	.627	.928	−1.84
Avoid contact	−1.270	−1.247	−.21
Benefit of doubt	.256	.646	−2.39*
Hesitate shooting	.122	.463	−2.10*
Good old boy	−.422	−.506	.43
Drugs and drinking	.268	−.354	3.65*
Violate rights	.795	.506	1.78
Freedom	.205	.072	.83
Community policing	−.679	−.753	.57
Males as officers	−1.284	−1.432	1.01
SALE			
Perception	−4.810	−7.040	2.66*

* = $p \leq .05$.

Note: T1 and T2 represent the distribution of the questionnaire. T1 was at the beginning of the semester and T2 was the end of the semester.

terms of the scale, Perception, students' perceptions were initially positive and became more positive at the end of the semester (−4.81 and −7.04) and were statistically significant ($p < .05$). (See Table 10.2.)

Finally, since gender and ethnicity have been linked to differences in citizens' perceptions of policing, an analysis for the scale, Perception, was completed to examine what affect, if any, gender and ethnicity had on perceptions. In addition, keeping in mind that "time" could also be important to changes in perceptions, a Repeated Measure Analysis was employed.

Regarding gender, its impact was statistically significant ($p < .05$) for the Perception scale. In all instances, prior, after, and overall, females had a more positive perception of policing than males. With respect to the changes over time, although time in itself is significant, the interaction between time and gender was not. Therefore, gender's affect on perceptions is relative to just gender and not to time. (See Table 10.3.)

Table 10–3 Repeated Measure Analysis, Gender and Ethnicity, For Scale–Perception.

	Mean (T1)	**Mean (T2)**	**Overall**
Males	−3.677	−4.871	−4.274
Females	−5.659	−8.683	−7.171
Entire Sample	−4.806	−7.042	−5.924
Between-Subjects (gender)	F value	3.88*	
Within-Subject (time)	F value	6.19*	
Gender by Time	F value	1.17	
	Mean (T1)	**Mean(T2)**	**Overall**
Whites	−7.277	−7.766	−7.522
Nonwhites	−.160	−5.680	−2.990
Entire Sample	−4.806	−7.042	−5.924
Between-Subjects (ethnicity)	F value	9.78*	
Within-Subject (time)	F value	12.19*	
Ethnicity by Time	F value	9.03*	

On the other hand, there was an interaction between ethnicity (whites and nonwhites) and time, where perceptions of nonwhite students changed significantly from a negative perspective to a more positive perspective. This indicated that ethnicity is also linked to perceptions, but in this case, the time factor is significant. (See Table 10.3).

DISCUSSION

Previous research indicates that citizens have various perceptions about policing. Sources that help perpetuate these perceptions include personal experiences and media representations. Although there seems to be research that examines these perceptions and how they might differ, there appears to be little research that focuses on how these perceptions could be changed. Research on perceptions of policing among college students, especially those enrolled in police-oriented classes, is nonexistent. This research is a step toward alleviating this shortcoming. Furthermore, it examined what those perceptions were coming into a class and whether those perceptions could be changed—for the better, it is hoped—by the end of the course.

The results found that initial perceptions were not very positive. However, at the completion of the course, reported perceptions were more positive. This was particularly true for nonwhite students, who initially were much more negative than their white classmates. With respect to gender, females had more positive perceptions than males, both initially and at the end. In either case, perceptions did change for the better. The question that arises at this point is: Did these perceptions change because of class content or because of time?

Based on the analyses employed, we can only speculate that course content over time did assist in changing initial perceptions. Unfortunately, since a comparison group, one not from a police course, was not used, we are unable to methodologically support our suggestion that the course content is a major contributor to changing student perceptions. However, this research did provide a starting point for further research.

REFERENCES

Alpert, G. P., and R. G. Dunham. 1986. Community policing. *Journal of Police Science and Administration* 14(3):212–22.

Carte, G. E. 1973. Changes in public attitudes toward the police: A comparison of 1938 and 1971 surveys. *Journal of Police Science and Administration* 1(2):182–200.

Decker, S. H. 1981. Citizens attitudes toward the police: A review of past findings and suggestions for future policy. *Journal of Police Science and Administration* 9(1):80–87.

———. 1985. The police and the public: Perceptions and policy recommendations. In *Police and law enforcement*, vol. 3, edited by R. J. Homant and D. B. Kennedy. 89–105. New York: AMS Press.

Gallop Poll Monthly (March 1991):53–56.

Glauser, M. J., and W. L. Tullar. 1985. Communicator style of police officers and citizen satisfaction with officer/citizen telephone conversations. *Journal of Police Science and Administration* 13(1):70–77.

Leff, D. R., D. L. Protess, and S. C. Brooks. 1986. Crusading journalism: Changing public attitudes and policy making agendas. *Public Opinion Quarterly* 50(3):300–15.

Mayhill, P. D., T. Barker, and R. D. Hunter. 1995. *Police-community relations and the administration of justice.* 4th ed. Englewood Cliffs, NJ: Prentice-Hall.

Meagher, S. 1985. Police patrol styles: How pervasive is community variation? *Journal of Police Science and Administration* 13(1):36–45.

Murty, K. S., J. B. Roebuck, and J. D. Smith. 1990. The image of the police in black Atlanta communities. *Journal of Police Science and Administration* 17(4):250–57.

O'Brien, J. T. 1978. Public attitudes toward police. *Journal of Police Science and Administration* 6(3):303–10.

Radelet, L. A. 1987. *Police and the community.* 4th ed. Englewood Cliffs, NJ: Macmillan.

Radelet, L. A., and D. Carter. 1994. *Police and the community.* 5th ed. Englewood Cliffs, NJ: Prentice-Hall.

Scaglion, R., and R. G. Condon. 1980. Determinants of attitudes toward city police. *Criminology* 17(4):485–94.

Walklate, S. 1992. Jack and Jill join up at Sunhill: Public images of police officers. *Policing and Society* 2:219–32.

---

1   The six statements that were not used in the scale were those that dealt with Professionalism, Decision making, Hesitating, Freedom, Community Policing, and Males as officers (Statements 10, 13, 14, 18, 19, and 20).

2   Readers should note that of these eight items, two—professionalism and hesitate shooting—were among the six items left off the scale.

Appendix

Students' Perceptions of Policing

This survey was designed to examine students' perceptions of policing prior to taking and after completing an introductory-level police course. Please read statement and without spending too much time "analyzing" the statement, indicate your level of agreement/disagreement using the scale provided. Thank you for your cooperation.

Strongly Disagree	Disagree	Not Sure	Agree	Strongly Agree
−2	−1	0	1	2

−2 −1 0 1 2   (1)   Although police officers are often called upon to do a variety of tasks, their primary role is crimefighter.

−2 −1 0 1 2   (2)   Most police officers do not solve more crimes because they are incompetent.

−2 −1 0 1 2   (3)   The motto "to Protect and Serve" is merely a public relations concept and has nothing to do with what police officers actually do.

−2 −1 0 1 2   (4)   At some point in their careers, all police officers commit a corrupt act.

−2 −1 0 1 2   (5)   Police officers are quicker to physically strike a minority group member than a white person.

−2 −1 0 1 2   (6)   Ignoring the needs of citizens is a common action of police officers.

−2 −1 0 1 2   (7)   Preventing crimes for rich, white people is more important to police officers than solving crimes for or assisting any ethnic or cultural group member.

−2 −1 0 1 2 (8) Police officers are only out to hurt or harass people instead of being out to help them.

−2 −1 0 1 2 (9) A problem people have with police officers is that they know police always out there, but they never know what to expect from them.

−2 −1 0 1 2 (10) Although policing is not a profession, most police officers are extremely professional.

−2 −1 0 1 2 (11) Many individuals who become police officers want to help society.

−2 −1 0 1 2 (12) Any time you see a police officer you should try to avoid having contact with him or her.

−2 −1 0 1 2 (13) Because police officers often have to make decisions with little time to think through the problem, they should be given the benefit of the doubt when they make a mistake.

−2 −1 0 1 2 (14) Police officers should never hesitate to shoot someone threatening their lives.

−2 −1 0 1 2 (15) The reason police officers are still primarily white males is because of politics, discrimination, and the "good old boy" system of recruitment.

−2 −1 0 1 2 (16) Police officers who take drugs or drink on duty should be immediately fired instead of being offered counseling or other assistance.

-2 -1 0 1 2 (17) No matter what the circumstances, if a police officer violates an individual's constitutional rights s/he should be held accountable.

-2 -1 0 1 2 (18) Most police officers are well-trained, educated individuals who should be given more freedom to use their commonsense to solve problems.

-2 -1 0 1 2 (19) Community policing is a bad idea because most police officers do not have the "skills" or "tools" necessary to make it work.

-2 -1 0 1 2 (20) Only males should be police officers because they are more physically and psychologically able to do the job.

Please provide the following information:

Gender: Male _____   Female _____

Race/Ethnicity: White _____   African American _____
Hispanic _____   Other _____

Age: _____

Year in College: Freshman _____   Sophomore _____
Junior _____   Senior _____   Other _____

Major: _____   Minor: _____

Other than Intro to Criminal Justice, have you taken any other courses with a police component? Yes _____   No _____

If Yes, how many? _____

Employment Goal: Law Enforcement _____
Probation _____   Courts _____   Corrections _____
Law _____   Other _____

Are you related to a police officer?
Yes _____   No _____
     If Yes, what is the relationship? _____

Last four digits of social security number (for analysis purposes only) _____

11

The Influence of Race on Prison Sentences for Murder in Twentieth-Century Texas

Deon E. Brock, Jon Sorensen, and James W. Marquart

PREFACE

The purpose of this study is to determine if race influenced punishment during the middle of this century. Studies from that time period are inconclusive and contradictory, mainly because of a failure to simultaneously control for other possibly influential variables. With data from Texas, analysis of variance (ANOVA) is used to determine if offenders' race influences the length of prison sentences for the crime of murder during 1923–1972. In order to control for many variables simultaneously while ascertaining the influence of race on sentence length, a multivariate statistical technique was needed that could accommodate categorical independent variables and a continuous dependent variable. ANOVA was chosen as the most appropriate test to use in determining if group means on a dependent variable are equal when the dependent

211

variable is interval level, and one or more categorical variables, or factors, define the groups. Controlling for a number of variables using this method, race of offender appears to affect prison sentence, with black offenders receiving more lenient sentences during the fifty-year period. The effects, however, are not invariant throughout the time period studied. During the 1920s and 1930s, African-American murderers were sentenced to longer periods of incarceration than whites, while sentences equalized in the 1940s, and whites received longer sentences in the 1950s through the early 1970s.

INTRODUCTION

Americans of African descent have been the victims of many forms of discrimination since their forced introduction to this country. This is especially true of the criminal law in general and corrections in particular. In the antebellum South, states enacted many laws to protect the institution of slavery. During the era of slavery, it was not a crime for a master to kill or injure a slave. At the same time, slaves who committed violations against whites received immediate, harsh, corporal, or capital punishment (Hindus 1980). An 1816 Georgia statute provided a mandatory death penalty for slaves or "freemen of colour" for the rape or attempted rape of a white female (Bowers 1984, 140). The same statute reduced the maximum sentence for white males from seven to two years and removed hard labor. Whites convicted of raping blacks were fined and/or imprisoned at the discretion of the court. Punishment in the South during the era of slavery served the purpose of minority-group oppression and majority-group protection through the differential creation and application of sanctions to slaves and free blacks versus whites.

After the Civil War, white dominance was maintained by the passage of so called "black codes." Newly formed prison systems in the South were populated almost entirely by former slaves. While Northern prisons were moving toward the reformatory model of indeterminate sentencing and training, southern prisons typically leased out their charges to rebuild infrastructure or set them to toil on plantation-style prison farms (McKelvey 1936). When black codes no longer had legal force, white southerners resorted to informal methods of asserting their authority through such actions as segregation, the creation of terrorist groups, and lynching.

Lynching, at its height around the turn of this century, served as the most malevolent among informal means of asserting social distance between blacks and whites in order to protect whites' status and power from blacks (Raper 1969; Teeters and Hedblum 1967). So effective was this informal sanction in the early-twentieth century that blacks often confessed to crimes out of fear of mob violence. The apparent symbiosis between extra-legal and legal forms of "justice" did not end with the confessions. Although an extra-legal affair, lynching was often sanctioned by, and even carried out by, local criminal justice officials. In addition, racial disparities in state-sanctioned executions and prison sentences for murder were quite glaring in the early-twentieth century (Garfinkel 1949; Johnson 1941; Marquart, Ekland-Olson, and Sorensen 1994).

There is little doubt that the past function of the criminal law has an effect on the modern function of the law. Historical patterns in the application of the criminal law are somewhat resistant to change. Extra-legal factors, including race of the offender, are still suggested to be strong determinants of how and when the law is applied (Black 1976, 1979; Hawkins 1983; Holmes and Daudistel 1984). Recent research indicates a disproportionately higher number of blacks than whites incarcerated, as well as higher rates of incarceration among blacks than whites (Arthur 1994; Flanagan, et al. 1991; Heaney 1991). The Sentencing Project has issued a report that showed the extent of this differential in 1992–93: "African-Americans are incarcerated at a rate that is more than six times that of whites—1,947 per 100,000, compared to 306 per 100,000" (Mauer 1994). While researchers agree on the presence of disparity, their explanations vary. While some take this level of disparity as evidence of "differential treatment" or biased application of the existing laws, others conclude that such disparity results from "differential involvement" in the sorts of crimes that typically result in prison sentences (Blumstein 1982; Hindelang 1982; Langan 1985). According to these authors, African Americans are much more often involved in interpersonal violent offenses, the kinds of crimes most likely to result in long prison terms.

Studies analyzing the sentencing of murderers in recent years have found little evidence of overt offender-based racial discrimination in the sentencing of murderers. A number of researchers have even reported anomalous findings wherein blacks are treated more leniently than whites (Bullock 1961; Kleck 1981). This apparent anomaly does not, however, rule out the influence of race (Peterson and Hagan 1984). According to Hawkins (1987), the nature of racial bias in sentencing has simply changed in recent years, becoming more institutionalized and subtle. Studies that control for a large number of variables are less likely to find evidence of racial discrimination because many of the legally relevant factors included in the analyses (e.g., prior record) are closely aligned with race. A large amount of research on capital punishment in the past two decades has shown the influence of race of offender to be limited primarily to the pretrial stages of the process as opposed to the sentencing stage and usually limited to its interaction with race of the victim (U.S. GAO 1991).

A gap exists, however, between studies of sentencing practices early in this century, which consistently found evidence of racial discrimination, and more recent studies from the past two decades, which have generally not found overt offender-based racial discrimination in sentencing. Studies completed during the middle of the century produced a body of inconsistent and inconclusive findings. Results depended upon geographical location, the types of legally relevant control variables, and the sorts of analyses performed. Most of the studies completed during the middle of this century did not include many controls, but simply presumed from racial disparities that discrimination was present (U.S.

Department of Justice 1974). Studies most often performed only simple cross-tabular analyses to determine whether significant relationships existed between race and sentence (Bridge and Mosure 1961; Johnson 1957). It is also difficult to generalize research findings based on samples from one city (Bensing and Schroeder 1960), or limited time frames (Bullock 1961). Later studies using more advanced statistical techniques to control for legal factors were less likely to find evidence of overt offender-based racial discrimination present in data from the middle of the century (Judson et al., 1967; Farrell and Swigert 1978; Kleck 1981).

At some point during the middle of this century, then, overt, offender-based, racial discrimination in the sentencing of murderers seems to have disappeared. Whether the reason for this disappearance is real or an artifact of the sophistication of the analyses employed has yet to be determined. The remainder of this article is devoted to an analysis of data from the middle of this century using multivariate analyses to simultaneously examine the interaction among, and influence of, some key variables on the sentencing of murderers. Our intention is to determine if unexplained racial disparities in the sentencing of murderers persist when relevant control variables are included in multivariate analyses, and also to determine if the patterns of disparity during the time-frame studied are static.

METHODS

In order to determine how race influenced punishment, to what extent, and its duration of influence, one southern prison system serves as a case study. For this study, data were collected from ledgers kept by the Texas Prison System. Information from the ledgers, including date of conviction, county of conviction, date received, offense, plea, race/ethnicity, sex, age, form of release, and date of release, was recorded on all inmates received for murder during 1923–1972. The sample actually represents a population of all offenders sentenced to prison for murder during a fifty-year period. For the purpose of the current study, the sample was limited only to African Americans and whites, excluding Native Americans and Hispanics, who had committed first-degree murder (N = 6,635).

The dependent variable is the maximum number of years that offenders were sentenced to serve in prison. In this variable, ranging from 5 to 99, life was coded as 99 years, because the Texas prison system has historically treated the life and 99-year terms as synonymous. In its original form, the variable is excessively skewed, with over one-quarter of the cases falling into the 99-year category; hence, the mean sentence length should be interpreted cautiously. For the statistical analyses, the logarithm of sentence length had to be used in order not to violate the assumption of linearity.

The main independent variable of interest is race of offenders. Other theoretically relevant variables present in the data set are plea, age, sex, and location. Plea is included because several studies have shown that those who plead guilty are likely to receive leniency. Those who do not plead guilty in essence receive a "trial tax" for wasting the time and cost of a criminal trial (McCarthy and Lindquist 1985). Offender's age and sex are important because younger offenders and females traditionally receive more lenient sentences due to less extensive criminal records and chivalry. These three variables have also been shown to interact with race in sentencing decisions. African Americans may be less likely to plea bargain than whites, which would partially explain their longer sentences (Petersilia 1985; Zatz 1985). If youthful or female African Americans are given relatively harsher sentences than youthful or female whites, this may signal an unwillingness to consider mitigating circumstances when minorities commit murder (Bowers 1984). Location indicates whether defendants were convicted in one of Texas' major urban counties—Bexar (San Antonio), Dallas, Harris (Houston), Tarrant (Fort Worth), and Travis (Austin)—versus a rural county. The more urbanized courts, and hence more bureaucratized, the more lenient are the sentences likely to be imposed (Hagan 1977). Further, in a more bureaucratized court, chances of discrimination are diminished so that sentencing disparities should be at a minimum in urban centers.

ANALYSIS

In most of the early studies completed on sentencing disparities, few used inferential statistics and even fewer controlled for the effects of other possibly influential variables. Early studies produced inconsistent results because researchers based conclusions primarily on the appearance of frequencies, percentages, and proportion tables. Among those who used inferential statistics to standardize determination of effects, chi-square was the predominant method. These simple bivariate statistical techniques could not account for relationships among variables and rule out the potential influence of rival causal factors.

Analysis of variance (ANOVA) is the statistical technique that was chosen herein to test the null hypotheses of no difference in prison sentence length among African Americans and whites. ANOVA is the most appropriate test to use to determine if group means on the dependent variable are equal when the dependent variable is continuous and one or more categorical variables, or factors, define the groups. In other words, ANOVA is most appropriate when researchers are interested in determining if significant differences exists among groups, defined by nominal-level independent variables, on an interval-level dependent variable. ANOVA compares the variance within each group (the average squared deviation of individual scores from the group mean on the dependent variable) to the variance between groups (the average squared deviation of group means from the grand mean). An F-Test of significance is calculated by dividing the within-group variance into the between-group variance. At infinite degrees of freedom, an F score of 1.0 or less indicates that the differences in scores within each group is as large or larger than the differences in scores between groups. At an extreme, all of the variance on the dependent variable would be within the groups, while the groups would all have exactly the same mean. In this case, the null hypothesis that the group means on the dependent variable are equal cannot be rejected. An F score larger than 1.0 indicates that the differences in scores between the groups is larger than the differences in scores within the groups. At an extreme, all variance would be between the means of the groups, while all scores within each group would be equal to that group's mean. Whether the F value is large enough to reject the null hypothesis of no difference between group means (statistically significant) on the dependent variable depends on the degrees of freedom and the chosen probability level.

Although much more advanced analyses of variance (i.e., those including multiple dependent variables or covariates— interval-level independent variables) may be performed, herein we use a relatively simple form with categorical predictor variables and one interval-level dependent variable. In Table 11.1, the mean prison sentence length is compared separately for the groups on each independent variable (bivariate one-way analyses of variance). While the raw means for sentence length are presented in Table 11.1, recall that the dependent variable had to be logarithmically transformed in order to meet ANOVAs assumption of linearity. Hence, all other numbers reported in Tables 11.1 and 11.2 (F values, significance, adjusted deviations, and betas) are based on the logged prison sentence variable.

Since multiple independent variables and significant two-way interactions are considered simultaneously (multivariate two-way analysis of variance) in the equation presented in Table 11.2, Multiple Classification Analysis is used to show the strength and direction of deviations for each category of the factors included in the model. The adjusted deviations presented in the first column of Table 11.2 show the distance of each category's mean from the grand (overall) mean not explained by the influence of other factors. The Betas in the second column of Table 11.2 are simply standardized regression coefficients, while the F values and associated levels of significance refer to the unadjusted deviations. R^2 has the same interpretation as in multiple regression, being the proportion of variance in the dependent variable accounted for by all of the factors and interaction terms.

FINDINGS

The analyses presented in Table 11.1 show that over the fifty-year period, African Americans received less severe sentences than whites. On average, whites received maximum sentences nearly ten years longer than African Americans, 39.7 years compared to 30.0 years. Other unexpected findings were those for plea and location. Those individuals pleading guilty and those convicted in urban areas received longer sentences. One expected finding was that females received leniency: males' average sentence was

Table 11-1 The Relationship among Predictor Variables and Sentence Length for First-Degree Murderers in Texas, 1923–1972.

Variables	Mean Length of Sentence	F	Sig.	Total
RACE		116.24	.00	
African American	30.0			3,987
White	39.7			2,648
PLEA		19.70	.00	
Guilty	36.1			2,927
Not Guilty	32.1			3,702
AGE		3.19	.07	
Under 25	35.2			1,195
25 and Over	33.1			4,196
SEX		90.18	.00	
Male	35.1			6,131
Female	19.2			504
LOCATION		50.15	.00	
Urban	38.2			2,289
Rural	31.6			4,346

nearly twice that of females, 35.1 years compared to 19.2 years. Although younger offenders appeared to have received slightly longer sentences, the finding was not significant at the .05 probability level.

To more adequately isolate the effects of race on sentence length, all factors were considered simultaneously in Table 11.2. With all of the other factors held constant, race of the defendant still exerted a significant influence on the length of prison sentence. Whites received much longer terms of imprisonment than blacks for murder in Texas during 1923–1972. All other factors considered, the effect of being African American on sentencing was a .12 decrease in logged prison years from the grand mean, while being white meant a sentence .17 logged years longer than the grand mean, an overall difference of nearly 10% (.29/2.84) lengthier prison sentences for whites than African Americans. Some two-way interactions with race were also significant, race by plea and race by age. For African Americans, pleading guilty or being under the age of twenty-five acted as mitigators, while for whites the opposite effect was observed. As in the bivariate analyses presented in Table 11.1, males received longer sentences than females, as did those who pled guilty and those convicted in urban counties, while age was not significant.

Some additional findings are of relevance concerning race and punishment for murder. First, although whites were given sentences 32% longer on average—prior to being adjusted or logged—than African Americans, African Americans ended up serving a much larger portion of their sentence. The average time served was 6.13 years for whites versus 5.9 years for African Americans, a difference of only 4%. Second, the effects of race are not invariant over the course of the fifty-year period studied. Prior to World War II, African Americans actually received significantly longer sentences than whites. ANOVAS (not reported) calculated for each decade show that sentences were longer for African Americans than whites in the 1920s and 1930s, with sentences being equal during the 1940s; and for the remainder of the period, 1950s to

Table 11–2 Analysis of Variance and Multiple-Classification Analysis for Factors Relating to Length of Sentence (Logged) for First-Degree Murderers in Texas, 1923–1972.

Main Effects	Adjusted Deviations	Beta	F	Sign. of F
RACE		.12	74.04	.00
African Americans	−.12			
White	.17			
PLEA		.05	14.02	.00
Guilty	.09			
Not Guilty	−.04			
AGE		.01	.66	.42
Under 25	.02			
25 and Over	−.01			
SEX		.11	73.12	.00
Male	.04			
Female	−.50			
LOCATION		.15	131.91	.00
Urban	.29			
Rural	−.12			
2-Way Interactions				
RACE by PLEA			9.89	.00
African American guilty	−.04			
African American not guilty	−.14			
White guilty	.43			
White not guilty	.07			
RACE by AGE			7.53	.01
African American under 25	−.17			
African American 25 and over	−.09			
White under 25	.36			
White 25 and over	.11			

Grand Mean = 2.84
Multiple R = .225; Multiple R^2 = .051

222 Practical Applications for Criminal Justice Statistics

early 1970s, whites received longer prison sentences than African Americans.

CONCLUSIONS

The analyses appear to support a nondiscriminatory interpretation of the sentencing of murderers in Texas in the mid-twentieth century. The seemingly anomalous findings that African Americans are given more lenient sentences than whites can be partially accounted for by the time period under study. Using one consistent multivariate statistical technique on the same set of data it was determined that a change did occur over the fifty-year time period studied. Consistent with the literature, during the early half of the century (1920s to 1930s) race of offender influenced sentencing in the predicted direction, African Americans receiving longer prison sentences than whites. Also consistent with the literature, this pattern changed so that whites were receiving longer sentences than African Americans during the second half of the century (1950s to 1970s). These findings suggest that the gap between research from the early-twentieth century and the past couple of decades is not a mere function of the statistical technique employed. Using several control variables in ANOVA, racial disparities in the early part of the century did not wash away.

The apparently anomalous findings that whites were sentenced to longer periods than African Americas during the second half of the century could indicate two possibilities. The first is that racial discrimination in sentencing no longer exists. While the past social control function of the criminal law held out through the Depression, by the WWII years historical patterns of racial discrimination in sentencing may have been reversed. This explanation, however, does not account for longer terms being received by whites during the second half of the century. The second possibility is that racial discrimination in sentencing still exists, but has become more institutionalized and subtle. With the burgeoning civil rights movement in the 1950s, it became clear that overt offender-based racial disparities in sentencing would not be tolerated. Although not included in our analysis, recent research has found pronounced disparities based on the race of the victim; the form of discrimination has changed. Further, blacks in recent years make up a larger proportion of those responsible for serious violent crimes and hence a greater proportion of the prison population. Whatever factors encourage a much higher rate of homicide among blacks than whites in recent years may be the result of institutionalized discrimination (e.g., ghettoization of inner cities, lack of opportunity). While not receiving as lengthy prison terms as whites, a much larger proportion of blacks incarcerated for murder during the latter half of the century could indicate that the criminal law is still fulfilling its social control function, even while sentencing studies in recent years are failing to find evidence of overt offender-based racial discrimination.

REFERENCES

Arthur, J. A. 1994. Correctional ideology of black correctional officers. *Federal Probation* 58:57–66.

Bensing, R. C., and O. J. Schroeder. 1960. *Homicide in an urban community.* Springfield, IL: Charles C. Thomas.

Black, D. 1976. *The behavior of law.* New York: Academic Press.

———. 1979. Common sense in the sociology of law. *American Sociological Review* 44:18–27.

Blumstein, A. 1982. On the racial disproportionality of United States' prison populations. *Journal of Criminal Law and Criminology* 73:1259–68.

Bowers, W. J. 1984. *Legal homicide: Death as punishment in America, 1864–1982.* Boston: Northeastern University Press.

Bridge, F. M., and J. Mosure. 1961. *Capital punishment.* Columbus: Ohio Legislative Service Commission.

Bullock, H. A. 1961. Significance of the racial factor in the length of prison sentences. *Journal of Criminal Law, Criminology, and Police Sciences* 52:411–17.

Farrell, R. A., and V. L. Swigert. 1978. Legal dispositions of inter-group and intra-group homicides. *Sociological Quarterly* 19:565–76.

Flanagan T. J., D. D. Clark, D. W. Aziz, and B. P. Szelest. 1991. Compositional changes in a long-term prisoner population: 1956–1989. *Prison Journal* 80:15–34.

Garfinkel, H. 1949. Research note on inter- and intra-racial homicide. *Social Forces* 27: 369–81.

Hagan, J. 1977. Criminal justice in rural and urban communities: A study of bureaucratization of justice. *Social Forces* 55:597–612.

Hawkins, D. F. 1983. Black and white homicide differentials: Alternatives to an inadequate theory. *Criminal Justice and Behavior* 10:407–40.

Hawkins, D. F. 1987. Beyond anomalies: Rethinking the conflict perspective on race and criminal punishment. *Social Forces* 65:719–45.

Heaney, G. W. 1991. The reality of guidelines sentencing: No end to disparity. *American Criminal Law Review* 28:161–232.

Hindelang, M. J. 1978. Race and involvement in common law personal crimes. *American Sociological Review* 43:93–109.

Hindus, M. S. 1980. *Prison and plantation: Crime, justice, and authority in Massachusetts and South Carolina, 1767–1878.* Chapel Hill: University of North Carolina Press.

Holmes, M. D., and H. C. Daudistel. 1984. Ethnicity and justice in the Southwest: The sentencing of Anglo, Black, and Mexican origin defendants. *Social Science Quarterly* 85:265–77.

Johnson, E. H. 1957. Selective factors in capital punishment. *Social Forces* 36:165–69.

Johnson, G. 1941. The Negro and crime. *Annals of the American Academy of Political and Social Sciences* 217:93–104.

Judson, C. J., J. J. Pandell, J. B. Owens, J. B. McIntosh, D. L. Matschullat. 1967. A study of the California jury in first-degree murder cases. *Stanford Law Review* 21:1297–1431.

Kleck, G. 1981. Racial discrimination in criminal sentencing: A critical evaluation of the evidence with additional evidence on the death penalty. *American Sociological Review* 46:783–805.

Langan, P. A. 1985. Racism on trial: New evidence to explain the racial composition of prisons in the United States. *Journal of Criminal Law and Criminology* 76:666–83.

Mauer, M. 1994. *Americans behind bars: The international uses of incarceration, 1992–1993.* Washington DC: The Sentencing Project.

Marquart, J. W., S. Ekland-Olson, and J. R. Sorensen. 1994. *The rope, the chair, and the needle.* Austin: University of Texas Press.

McCarthy, B. R., and C. A. Lindquist. 1985. Certainty of punishment and sentence in mitigation in plea behavior. *Justice Quarterly* 2:363–83.

McKelvey, B. 1936. *American prisons.* Chicago: University of Chicago Press.

Petersilia, J. 1985. Racial disparities in the criminal justice system: A summary. *Crime and Delinquency* 31:15–34.

Peterson, R. D., and J. Hagan. 1984. Changing conceptions of race: Towards an account of anomalous findings of sentencing research. *American Sociological Review* 49:56–70.

Raper, A. F. 1969. *The tragedy of lynching.* Chapel Hill: University of North Carolina Press.

Teeters, N., and J. Hedblum. 1967. *Hang by the neck: The legal use of scaffold and noose, gibbet, stake, and firing squad from colonial times to present.* Springfield, IL: Charles C. Thomas.

United States Department of Justice. 1974. *Capital punishment, 1971–1972.* Washington, DC: USGPO.

United States Government Accounting Office. 1991. *Death penalty sentencing: research indicates pattern of racial disparities.* Washington, DC: USGAO.

Zatz, M. J. 1985. Pleas, priors, and prison: Racial/ethnic difference in sentencing. *Social Science Research* 14:169–93.

Index

effect of learning disabilities,
64
expected level of
achievement, 63
summary, 66–67
method
data analysis, 55–57
procedure, 54
results, 57–61
subjects, 53–54
tests administered, 54–55

K

Kentucky
drug-testing programs for
community corrections in
compared with testing
programs in other cities, 36,
37(f)–38(f), 39
description of, 27–28
methods, 28–29
purpose of, 28
recidivism rates for offenders
testing positive and referred
for treatment *vs.* those testing
negative for drug abuse, 39–
42
research findings
client attributes associated
with substance abuse, 30,
32–33
cocaine use
client attributes associated
with, 33
and likelihood of
completing Kentucky
Substance Abuse
Program, 42–43
patterns of, 30, 31(f)
marijuana use
client attributes associated
with, 32–33
patterns of, 30, 31(f)
variables that predicted,
on first drug test,
36

substance abuse patterns,
29–30, 30(f)
variables that predicted
cocaine abuse on first drug
test
for blacks, 35
for whites, 34–35
variables that predicted
failure on first drug test
for blacks, 34
for whites, 33–34
variables that predicted
multiple drug abuse on
first drug test
for blacks, 35–36
for whites, 35
results, 26–27
marijuana cultivation, 43–44
Kentucky Substance Abuse Program
(KSAP)
recidivism rates for offenders
testing positive and referred for
treatment *vs.* those testing
negative for drug abuse, 39–
42
treatment program findings, 26
variables that predicted
completion of, 42–43
King, Gregory, 6
KSAP. *See* Kentucky Substance
Abuse Program

L

Law Enforcement Assistance
Administration (LEAA), 14
LEAA. *See* Law Enforcement
Assistance Administration
Learning disabilities, effect on
academic achievement of
juvenile delinquents, 64
LePlay, Frederic, 9
Life tables, 6–7

M

MANOVA. *see* Multiple analysis of
variance

Other Criminal Justice Books from Butterworth-Heinemann

Criminal Justice Statistics: A Practical Approach by Arthur J. Lurigio, M.L. Dantzker, Magnus J. Seng, and James M. Sinacore
1996   296pp   0-7506-9672-9   hc $49.95

The Juvenile Justice System: Law and Process by Mary Clement
1996   345pp   0-7506-9810-1   hc $44.95

Criminal Justice: An Introduction by Philip P. Purpura
1996   400pp   0-7506-9630-3   pb $34.95

Comparative and International Criminal Justice Systems: Policing, Judiciary and Corrections by Obi N.I. Ebbe
1996   248pp   0-7506-9688-5   hc $44.95

The Art of Investigative Interviewing: A Human Approach to Testimonial Evidence by Charles L. Yeschke
1997   320pp   0-7506-9808-X   pb $29.95

African-American Perspectives: On Crime Causation, Criminal Justice, Administration, and Crime Prevention by Anne T. Sulton
1996   224pp   0-7506-9813-6   pb $24.95

Feel free to visit our web site at: http://www.bh.com

These books are available from all good bookstores or in case of difficulty call:
1-800-366-2665 in the U.S. or +44-1865-310366 in Europe.

E-Mail Mailing List

An e-mail mailing list giving information on latest releases, special promotions/ offe and other news relating to Butterworth-Heinemann Criminal Justice titles is availab To subscribe, send an e-mail message to majordomo@world.std.com. Include in messa body (not in subject line) subscribe bh-criminal-justice